Table of Content

The Nuclear Club: A Comprehensive Guide to Countries and Current Nuclear Capabilities

By Roberto Miguel Rodriguez

Chapter 1: Introduction to Dirty Bombs and Homeland Security Efforts

Introduction

In this book, we will explore the various sub-topics related to the nuclear field. The Nuclear Club: A Comprehensive Guide to Current Countries with Nuclear Capabilities aims to provide valuable insights and knowledge to the public, including individuals interested in the nuclear club, countries aspiring to develop nuclear capabilities, as well as those who have publicly renounced nuclear weapons.

The subchapter will delve into several crucial areas, starting with nuclear power plants and energy production. We will discuss the significance of nuclear energy as a source of power, its advantages, and challenges. Additionally, we will explore the countries with operational nuclear power plants and their energy production capacities.

Moving on, we will examine nuclear disarmament and non-proliferation efforts. Here, we will outline the international agreements and organizations dedicated to reducing and eliminating nuclear weapons. We will also discuss the challenges faced in achieving complete disarmament and the role of countries with nuclear capabilities in this process.

Next, we will explore the topic of nuclear weapons testing and development. This section will discuss the history of nuclear weapons testing, including notable incidents and their implications. We will also analyze the current state of nuclear weapons development in various countries and the potential consequences for global security.

Nuclear safety and emergency preparedness will be another crucial sub-topic. We will provide an overview of safety protocols and measures implemented in nuclear power plants to prevent accidents. Furthermore, we will discuss emergency preparedness plans and the lessons learned from major nuclear accidents such as Chernobyl and Fukushima.

The subchapter will also touch upon nuclear diplomacy and international relations. We will examine the role of nuclear weapons in shaping diplomatic strategies and international alliances. Moreover, we will analyze the impact of nuclear capabilities on global politics and security.

Nuclear deterrence and strategic stability will be explored in detail, focusing on the concept of deterrence and its role in maintaining peace. We will discuss the theories and doctrines associated with nuclear deterrence and its effectiveness in preventing conflicts.

Additionally, the subchapter will cover nuclear weapons delivery systems, including missiles, submarines, and bombers. We will analyze the advancements in technology and the implications for global security.

Furthermore, we will explore nuclear weapons modernization and technological advancements. This section will discuss the research and development efforts to enhance nuclear capabilities and the potential consequences for nuclear disarmament.

Nuclear espionage and intelligence gathering will be another key sub-topic. We will highlight instances of nuclear espionage and its impact on international relations. Furthermore, we will analyze the role of intelligence agencies in monitoring nuclear activities.

Finally, the subchapter will discuss nuclear accidents and incidents. We will examine significant incidents such as Chernobyl and Fukushima, their causes, consequences, and the lessons learned. This section will emphasize the importance of nuclear safety and emergency preparedness.

Overall, this subchapter aims to provide a comprehensive overview of the diverse aspects of the nuclear field. It is designed to educate and inform the public, as well as individuals interested in various niches within the nuclear club.

Understanding the Threat of Dirty Bombs

The threat of dirty bombs poses a significant risk to national security and the safety of our citizens. In this subchapter, we will delve into the intricacies of this threat, exploring the various factors involved in the making of a dirty bomb and the efforts undertaken by the Department of Homeland Security to prevent its creation by terrorists.

One of the key aspects to understanding this threat lies in comprehending the various nuclear materials detection and tracking technologies available. As security agents, it is essential to stay updated on the latest advancements in this field to effectively detect and intercept any potential threats.

Additionally, we will explore the security protocols in place for nuclear facilities and transportation. Ensuring the highest level of security for these facilities and transportation routes is crucial in preventing terrorists from acquiring the necessary materials to construct a dirty bomb.

In today's interconnected world, cybersecurity measures are of paramount importance. We will discuss the measures taken to prevent terrorist hacking of nuclear systems, as any breach in these systems could lead to catastrophic consequences.

Furthermore, we will explore radiation detection and monitoring strategies. By understanding these strategies, security agents can effectively identify and mitigate any radiation threats, ensuring a rapid response to potential dirty bomb incidents.

Intelligence gathering on terrorist organizations' interest in dirty bombs is another critical aspect to be addressed. By staying informed on their intentions and capabilities, security agents can proactively disrupt any plans before they come to fruition.

International cooperation and information sharing on nuclear threats are vital in addressing this global threat. We will examine the efforts made to collaborate with international partners to share intelligence and enhance our collective ability to prevent dirty bomb attacks.

Emergency response plans and preparedness for dirty bomb incidents are essential components of any comprehensive security strategy. We will delve into the best practices for developing robust emergency response plans, ensuring a coordinated and swift response in the event of a dirty bomb incident.

Public awareness campaigns play a significant role in preventing dirty bomb attacks. We will discuss the importance of educating the public about the dangers of dirty bombs and promoting vigilance and reporting of suspicious activities.

Legal frameworks and penalties for individuals involved in dirty bomb activities are crucial deterrents. We will explore the existing legal frameworks and the penalties associated with engaging in such activities, emphasizing the consequences for those involved.

Lastly, we will touch upon the ongoing research and development of advanced technologies aimed at enhancing our dirty bomb prevention efforts. Staying at the forefront of technological advancements is crucial to staying one step ahead of potential threats.

In conclusion, understanding the threat of dirty bombs is imperative for security agents. By comprehending the various aspects discussed in this subchapter, we can strengthen our efforts to prevent the creation of dirty bombs by terrorists and ensure the safety and security of our nation and its people.

The Role of the Department of Homeland Security

Introduction:

The Department of Homeland Security (DHS) plays a crucial role in safeguarding the United States from various threats, including the making of a dirty bomb. This subchapter will explore the efforts made by the DHS to prevent terrorists from acquiring and using nuclear materials, as well as the strategies and technologies employed to combat this threat.

Nuclear Materials Detection and Tracking Technologies:

One of the primary responsibilities of the DHS is to develop and implement advanced technologies for detecting and tracking nuclear materials. Through continuous research and development, the DHS aims to enhance the capabilities of its radiation detection systems, ensuring the timely identification of any illicit nuclear activities.

Security Protocols for Nuclear Facilities and Transportation:

To prevent terrorists from gaining access to nuclear materials, the DHS collaborates closely with nuclear facilities and transportation agencies to establish stringent security protocols. This includes thorough background checks for personnel, secure transportation methods, and the implementation of robust physical security measures at nuclear facilities.

Cybersecurity Measures to Prevent Terrorist Hacking:

Recognizing the potential for terrorists to exploit cyber vulnerabilities in nuclear systems, the DHS has prioritized cybersecurity measures. Through continuous monitoring and threat intelligence sharing, the DHS aims to prevent hackers from gaining unauthorized access to critical nuclear infrastructure.

Radiation Detection and Monitoring Strategies:

The DHS employs comprehensive radiation detection and monitoring strategies to identify any unusual radiation levels. By deploying mobile detection units and utilizing advanced sensors, the DHS can quickly respond to potential dirty bomb threats and mitigate the risks associated with radioactive materials.

Intelligence Gathering on Terrorist Interest in Dirty Bombs:

The DHS actively gathers intelligence on terrorist organizations' interest in dirty bombs. Through intelligence sharing with domestic and international partners, the DHS aims to stay ahead of potential threats and disrupt any activities related to the acquisition or production of a dirty bomb.

International Cooperation and Information Sharing:

Recognizing the global nature of nuclear threats, the DHS fosters international cooperation and information sharing on nuclear threats. By collaborating with foreign counterparts, the DHS can exchange best practices, enhance intelligence sharing, and collectively combat the proliferation of dirty bombs.

Emergency Response Plans and Preparedness:

The DHS develops comprehensive emergency response plans and conducts regular drills to ensure preparedness in the event of a dirty bomb incident. By coordinating with federal, state, and local agencies, the DHS aims to minimize the impact of such an incident and protect public safety.

Public Awareness Campaigns:

The DHS conducts public awareness campaigns to educate the general public about the dangers of dirty bombs. By raising awareness, the DHS aims to empower individuals to report suspicious activities and enhance overall preparedness within communities.

Legal Frameworks and Penalties:

The DHS works closely with law enforcement agencies and lawmakers to establish stringent legal frameworks and penalties for individuals involved in dirty bomb activities. By imposing severe consequences, the DHS aims to deter potential individuals from engaging in such dangerous activities.

Research and Development of Advanced Technologies:

The DHS invests in research and development to enhance dirty bomb prevention efforts. By exploring cutting-edge technologies, such as advanced sensors and detection systems, the DHS strives to stay ahead of evolving threats and continuously improve its capabilities.

Conclusion:

The DHS plays a vital role in preventing the making of a dirty bomb by terrorists. Through robust detection and monitoring technologies, security protocols, intelligence gathering, international cooperation, and public awareness campaigns, the DHS aims to safeguard the nation from this grave threat. By constantly adapting and innovating, the DHS stays at the forefront of efforts to enhance dirty bomb prevention and protect national security.

Chapter 2: Nuclear Materials Detection and Tracking Technologies

Current Technologies for Detecting Nuclear Materials

In the ongoing battle against terrorism and the threat of dirty bombs, the Department of Homeland Security (DHS) has made significant strides in developing and implementing cutting-edge technologies for the detection of nuclear materials. These technologies play a crucial role in safeguarding our nation's security and preventing the catastrophic consequences of a dirty bomb attack.

One of the primary focuses of DHS is the detection and tracking of nuclear materials. Advanced scanning devices and radiation detection systems are deployed at various entry points, such as airports, seaports, and border crossings, to identify any illicit movement of radioactive materials. These technologies utilize gamma-ray spectrometry, neutron activation analysis, and other techniques to accurately identify and quantify the presence of nuclear materials.

In addition to securing transportation routes, security protocols have been established for nuclear facilities and transportation. Enhanced access controls, rigorous background checks, and continuous monitoring are implemented to prevent unauthorized access and ensure the safety of these facilities. Furthermore, cybersecurity measures are in place to protect against potential terrorist hacking of nuclear systems, including firewalls, encryption, and regular vulnerability assessments.

The radiation detection and monitoring strategies employed by DHS involve the deployment of a network of sensors and detectors across the country. These sensors can quickly identify and locate any abnormal radiation levels, enabling a swift response to potential threats.

Additionally, intelligence gathering on terrorist organizations' interest in dirty bombs is a critical aspect of DHS efforts. By closely monitoring and analyzing communications, financial transactions, and other activities, intelligence agencies can identify potential threats and take proactive measures to prevent attacks.

International cooperation and information sharing are pivotal in combating the threat of dirty bombs. DHS collaborates with partner countries, sharing intelligence, best practices, and technological advancements to develop a comprehensive global defense against nuclear terrorism. This collaboration includes joint exercises, capacity-building programs, and the exchange of experts to enhance preparedness and response capabilities.

To ensure effective emergency response and preparedness for dirty bomb incidents, DHS has developed comprehensive plans and protocols. These plans outline the roles and responsibilities of various agencies, establish communication channels, and provide guidance on evacuation, decontamination, and medical treatment.

Public awareness campaigns are also integral to DHS efforts. By educating the public about the dangers of dirty bombs and the importance of vigilance, individuals can become the first line of defense in identifying and reporting suspicious activities. Additionally, legal frameworks and penalties have been established to deter individuals involved in dirty bomb activities.

Finally, research and development initiatives are continuously pursued to advance technologies and enhance prevention efforts. Improved detectors, remote sensing technologies, and data analytics are being explored to detect and track nuclear materials more efficiently and accurately.

In conclusion, the current technologies for detecting nuclear materials are crucial in the fight against dirty bombs. Through the implementation of advanced detection systems, security protocols, cybersecurity measures, intelligence gathering, international cooperation, and public awareness campaigns, DHS is working tirelessly to prevent the making of a dirty bomb by terrorists. However, the ongoing research and development efforts remain paramount in staying ahead of the evolving threat landscape and ensuring the security of our nation.

Advancements in Nuclear Materials Tracking

In recent years, the threat of a dirty bomb attack has become an increasing concern for security agents and the Department of Homeland Security. The potential devastation that a dirty bomb could cause is unimaginable, and as such, efforts to prevent terrorists from obtaining and using nuclear materials have intensified. Advancements in nuclear materials tracking have played a crucial role in these efforts, providing security agents with the tools and technology needed to detect and prevent the illicit trafficking of radioactive materials.

One of the key components of nuclear materials tracking is the development of advanced detection technologies. These technologies utilize various methods, such as radiation detectors and spectroscopy, to identify and analyze radioactive materials. The use of these technologies has significantly improved the ability to detect and track nuclear materials, both at nuclear facilities and in transportation. By implementing these detection systems, security agents can identify suspicious activities and intercept potential threats before they reach their intended targets.

In addition to detection technologies, security protocols for nuclear facilities and transportation have been enhanced to ensure the safe and secure handling of radioactive materials. These protocols include strict access control measures, background checks for personnel, and regular inspections of facilities and vehicles. By implementing these security measures, the risk of unauthorized access to nuclear materials is significantly reduced.

Cybersecurity measures have also been implemented to prevent terrorist hacking of nuclear systems. As technology advances, so does the risk of cyber-attacks. To counter this threat, nuclear facilities have implemented robust cybersecurity systems to protect their networks and prevent unauthorized access. Regular cybersecurity audits and training programs are conducted to ensure the highest level of protection against potential cyber threats.

Intelligence gathering on terrorist organizations' interest in dirty bombs has also been a priority for security agencies. Through international cooperation and information sharing, intelligence agencies are able to track and monitor the activities of terrorist groups and identify any potential threats related to dirty bombs. This information is crucial in preventing terrorist attacks and apprehending those involved in planning or attempting to acquire nuclear materials.

Emergency response plans and preparedness for dirty bomb incidents are also a critical aspect of nuclear materials tracking. By developing comprehensive response plans, security agencies can effectively respond to and mitigate the impact of a dirty bomb attack. These plans include coordination with local law enforcement, evacuation procedures, and medical response protocols. Regular drills and exercises are conducted to test the effectiveness of these plans and identify areas for improvement.

Public awareness campaigns have also been launched to educate the general public about the dangers of dirty bombs. By raising awareness about the potential consequences of a dirty bomb attack, individuals are more likely to report suspicious activities and cooperate with security agencies in their efforts to prevent such attacks.

Legal frameworks and penalties for individuals involved in dirty bomb activities have been strengthened to deter potential terrorists. Harsh penalties and strict enforcement of these laws serve as a strong deterrent and send a clear message that the acquisition and use of nuclear materials for terrorist purposes will not be tolerated.

Finally, research and development of advanced technologies continue to drive advancements in nuclear materials tracking. Scientists and engineers are constantly working on innovative solutions to enhance the prevention efforts of dirty bomb attacks. From improved detection technologies to more secure transportation methods, these advancements are essential in staying one step ahead of potential threats.

In conclusion, advancements in nuclear materials tracking have significantly improved the ability of security agents and the Department of Homeland Security to detect, track, and prevent the illicit trafficking of radioactive materials. From enhanced detection technologies to robust security protocols and international cooperation, these advancements are crucial in the fight against the making of a dirty bomb by terrorists. By staying vigilant, investing in research and development, and fostering international partnerships, security agents are better equipped to protect our nations from the devastating consequences of a dirty bomb attack.

Challenges in Detecting and Tracking Nuclear Materials

The threat of a dirty bomb looms large in today's world, and it is of utmost importance for security agents to understand the challenges associated with detecting and tracking nuclear materials. In this subchapter, we will explore the various hurdles faced by security agencies in their fight against the creation and use of dirty bombs.

One of the primary challenges in this regard is the advancement of nuclear materials detection and tracking technologies. Terrorist organizations are constantly evolving, and so are their methods of obtaining and hiding nuclear materials. Security agents must stay one step ahead by continuously innovating and improving their detection technologies to ensure that no potential threat goes unnoticed.

Another crucial aspect is the establishment of robust security protocols for nuclear facilities and transportation. These protocols must be strictly adhered to and include measures such as stringent background checks, surveillance systems, and secure transportation methods to prevent unauthorized access to nuclear materials.

Cybersecurity measures also play a crucial role in preventing terrorist hacking of nuclear systems. In today's interconnected world, digital vulnerabilities can be exploited by terrorists to gain access to sensitive information or disrupt critical infrastructure. Constant monitoring and upgrading of cybersecurity systems are necessary to counter this threat effectively.

Radiation detection and monitoring strategies are vital in identifying the presence of radioactive materials. However, the challenge lies in differentiating between naturally occurring radioactive sources and those used for nefarious purposes. Security agents must continuously enhance their knowledge and expertise in radiation detection to accurately identify potential threats.

Intelligence gathering on terrorist organizations' interest in dirty bombs is a critical aspect of prevention. Security agencies must collaborate with international partners to collect and share information on the activities and intentions of such organizations. This exchange of intelligence can provide valuable insights and aid in proactive measures to counter the threat.

International cooperation and information sharing on nuclear threats are equally important. The fight against dirty bombs is a global effort, and close collaboration between nations is necessary to combat this menace effectively. Joint exercises, information exchange platforms, and international agreements play a pivotal role in this regard.

Emergency response plans and preparedness for dirty bomb incidents are essential for minimizing the impact in case of an attack. Security agents must work closely with emergency response teams to develop comprehensive plans that encompass evacuation strategies, medical support, and containment measures to mitigate the consequences of a dirty bomb explosion.

Public awareness campaigns on the dangers of dirty bombs can also contribute significantly to prevention efforts. By educating the public about the risks associated with these weapons, individuals can become more vigilant and report suspicious activities, ultimately strengthening the overall security landscape.

Legal frameworks and penalties for individuals involved in dirty bomb activities are necessary to deter potential perpetrators. Strict regulations and severe consequences act as a deterrent and send a clear message that the creation and use of dirty bombs will not be tolerated.

Finally, research and development of advanced technologies are crucial to enhance dirty bomb prevention efforts. Constant innovation can lead to the discovery of new detection methods and materials that can significantly enhance security agents' ability to detect and track nuclear materials.

In conclusion, the challenges in detecting and tracking nuclear materials are multifaceted. However, by addressing these challenges head-on and adopting a proactive approach, security agents can effectively mitigate the threat of dirty bombs and safeguard the well-being of nations and their citizens.

Chapter 3: Security Protocols for Nuclear Facilities and Transportation

Physical Security Measures for Nuclear Facilities

Nuclear facilities are critical infrastructures that require robust physical security measures to prevent unauthorized access, sabotage, theft, and potential use of nuclear materials in the making of dirty bombs. The Department of Homeland Security (DHS) has been actively involved in developing and implementing security protocols to safeguard these facilities and prevent terrorist attacks. This subchapter will explore various physical security measures employed by nuclear facilities, aimed at ensuring the safety of nuclear materials and preventing their misuse by terrorists.

One of the primary physical security measures employed by nuclear facilities is access control. This involves the use of multiple layers of security, such as fences, barriers, and surveillance systems, to deter and detect unauthorized individuals attempting to gain entry. Highly trained security personnel are deployed at entrances and checkpoints to verify the identity and credentials of individuals, ensuring only authorized personnel have access.

In addition to access control, nuclear facilities employ advanced detection technologies to identify and track nuclear materials. These include radiation detection devices and monitoring systems that can quickly identify any unusual levels of radiation, signaling a potential threat. These systems are regularly tested and calibrated to ensure their accuracy and reliability.

To protect against cyber threats, nuclear facilities have implemented robust cybersecurity measures. These measures include firewalls, intrusion detection systems, and strict access controls to prevent unauthorized access to critical systems. Regular vulnerability assessments and penetration testing are conducted to identify and address any potential weaknesses in the cybersecurity infrastructure.

Intelligence gathering plays a crucial role in preventing the making of dirty bombs. Nuclear facilities work closely with intelligence agencies to gather information on terrorist organizations' interest in dirty bombs. This information is used to enhance security protocols and respond proactively to potential threats.

International cooperation and information sharing are vital in combating nuclear threats. Nuclear facilities collaborate with international partners, sharing information on emerging threats, best practices, and technological advancements. This collaboration fosters a global effort to prevent the making of dirty bombs.

Emergency response plans and preparedness are crucial in the event of a dirty bomb incident. Nuclear facilities have well-developed emergency response plans that include evacuation procedures, decontamination protocols, and coordination with local law enforcement and emergency management agencies.

Public awareness campaigns play a vital role in educating the public about the dangers of dirty bombs. Nuclear facilities actively engage with communities, conducting outreach programs, and disseminating information through various channels to raise awareness and promote vigilance.

Legal frameworks and penalties for individuals involved in dirty bomb activities act as a deterrent. Strict laws and severe penalties serve as a warning to potential perpetrators, ensuring that those involved in the making of dirty bombs face significant consequences.

Lastly, continuous research and development of advanced technologies are critical in enhancing dirty bomb prevention efforts. Nuclear facilities invest in cutting-edge technologies to improve detection capabilities, enhance physical security measures, and stay one step ahead of potential threats.

In conclusion, physical security measures employed by nuclear facilities are essential to prevent the making of dirty bombs. Through access control, detection technologies, cybersecurity measures, intelligence gathering, international cooperation, emergency preparedness, public awareness campaigns, legal frameworks, and research and development, nuclear facilities work tirelessly to protect nuclear materials and ensure the safety and security of our communities.

Transportation Security Protocols for Nuclear Materials

Transporting nuclear materials poses a significant threat to national security, as terrorists can exploit vulnerabilities in the transportation process to obtain these materials for the creation of dirty bombs. To counter this threat, robust transportation security protocols must be implemented to ensure the safe and secure transport of nuclear materials.

One of the key elements in transportation security protocols is the use of advanced detection and tracking technologies. These technologies enable security agents to identify and monitor the movement of nuclear materials, ensuring that they are not diverted or tampered with during transit. State-of-the-art radiation detection equipment plays a crucial role in this process, as it can identify the presence of radioactive materials and enable swift response measures.

In addition to detection technologies, cybersecurity measures are also vital to prevent terrorist hacking of nuclear systems. The Department of Homeland Security works tirelessly to develop and implement robust cybersecurity protocols to safeguard nuclear transportation systems from cyber threats. This includes the use of encryption, firewalls, and multi-factor authentication to protect against unauthorized access and potential sabotage.

Furthermore, intelligence gathering on terrorist organizations' interest in dirty bombs is paramount. Through close collaboration with intelligence agencies, security agents can stay one step ahead by identifying potential threats and taking proactive measures to prevent them. This includes monitoring online communications, tracking suspicious activities, and infiltrating terrorist networks to gather crucial information.

International cooperation and information sharing play a crucial role in addressing the threat of dirty bombs. By collaborating with other countries and sharing intelligence, security agents can enhance their understanding of global nuclear threats and develop effective countermeasures. This partnership also facilitates the exchange of best practices, technology sharing, and joint training exercises to improve transportation security protocols worldwide.

Emergency response plans and preparedness are essential components of transportation security protocols. Security agents must develop comprehensive plans to respond swiftly and effectively in the event of a dirty bomb incident. This includes establishing evacuation procedures, setting up decontamination sites, and coordinating with local law enforcement and emergency response teams.

Public awareness campaigns are crucial to educate the public about the dangers of dirty bombs and to encourage vigilance. By raising awareness, individuals can play a vital role in identifying and reporting suspicious activities, thus acting as an additional layer of defense against potential threats.

To deter individuals involved in dirty bomb activities, legal frameworks and penalties must be established. Strict laws should be enacted to punish those who engage in the creation, possession, or transport of dirty bombs. These penalties serve as a deterrent and send a strong message that such activities will not be tolerated.

Research and development of advanced technologies are ongoing in order to enhance dirty bomb prevention efforts. Continuous innovation is necessary to stay ahead of evolving threats and to develop more effective detection, tracking, and response systems. By investing in research and development, security agents can strengthen their capabilities and enhance the safety and security of nuclear material transportation.

In conclusion, transportation security protocols for nuclear materials are essential to safeguard against the threat of dirty bombs. By employing advanced detection and tracking technologies, implementing cybersecurity measures, gathering intelligence, fostering international cooperation, developing emergency response plans, raising public awareness, establishing legal frameworks, and investing in research and development, security agents can significantly enhance their ability to prevent the creation and transport of dirty bombs, thus ensuring the safety and security of nations around the world.

Ensuring Safety during Nuclear Material Transfers

The transfer of nuclear materials poses a significant risk if not handled with utmost care and security. In this subchapter, we will delve into the various measures and protocols that need to be in place to ensure the safety of nuclear material transfers. By understanding these procedures, security agents can effectively mitigate the risk of terrorists obtaining these materials and using them to create a dirty bomb.

One crucial aspect of ensuring safety during nuclear material transfers is the use of advanced detection and tracking technologies. By implementing state-of-the-art equipment, security agents can identify any attempts to tamper with or steal nuclear materials. These technologies, such as radiation detectors and tracking devices, enable real-time monitoring of the materials throughout the transfer process.

In addition to technological measures, security protocols play a vital role in safeguarding nuclear facilities and transportation. Strict access control, background checks, and comprehensive training for personnel involved in the transfer process are essential. By strictly adhering to these protocols, security agents can minimize the risk of insider threats and unauthorized access to nuclear materials.

In the digital age, cybersecurity measures are crucial to prevent terrorist hacking of nuclear systems. By implementing robust cybersecurity protocols, such as regular system updates, encryption, and intrusion detection systems, security agents can thwart any attempts to compromise the security of nuclear facilities and transportation networks.

Radiation detection and monitoring strategies are also key components of ensuring safety during nuclear material transfers. By deploying radiation detection devices at various checkpoints, security agents can identify any unauthorized presence of nuclear materials and respond promptly to potential threats.

Intelligence gathering on terrorist organizations' interest in dirty bombs is another critical aspect of preventing their creation. By actively monitoring and analyzing intelligence, security agents can identify potential threats and take appropriate preventive measures to counter them.

International cooperation and information sharing on nuclear threats are essential for comprehensive security. By collaborating with other countries, sharing intelligence, and collectively addressing nuclear threats, security agents can enhance their capabilities to prevent the making of dirty bombs.

Emergency response plans and preparedness for dirty bomb incidents are vital to minimize the consequences of an attack. By having well-coordinated response plans, including evacuation procedures, decontamination protocols, and medical assistance, security agents can effectively manage the aftermath of a dirty bomb incident.

Public awareness campaigns play a crucial role in educating the public about the dangers of dirty bombs. By disseminating information about the potential consequences of such attacks, security agents can enlist public support in preventing the creation and use of dirty bombs.

Legal frameworks and penalties for individuals involved in dirty bomb activities serve as deterrents. By enacting strict laws and imposing severe penalties, security agents can discourage individuals from engaging in any activities related to dirty bombs.

Finally, ongoing research and development of advanced technologies are essential to enhance dirty bomb prevention efforts. By investing in innovative solutions, security agents can stay ahead of emerging threats and continuously improve their ability to detect and prevent the making of dirty bombs.

In conclusion, ensuring safety during nuclear material transfers requires a multi-faceted approach that encompasses advanced technologies, security protocols, cybersecurity measures, intelligence gathering, international cooperation, emergency response plans, public awareness campaigns, legal frameworks, and continuous research and development. By diligently implementing these measures, security agents can effectively combat the threat of dirty bombs and protect national security.

Chapter 4: Cybersecurity Measures to Prevent Terrorist Hacking of Nuclear Systems

Vulnerabilities of Nuclear Systems to Cyberattacks

In today's interconnected world, the threat of cyberattacks has become increasingly prevalent, extending its reach to critical infrastructures such as nuclear systems. This subchapter aims to shed light on the vulnerabilities of nuclear systems to cyberattacks and the urgent need for robust cybersecurity measures to prevent potential terrorist hacking.

Nuclear facilities and transportation networks are prime targets for cybercriminals due to the catastrophic consequences that could result from a successful attack. The potential of a dirty bomb, a conventional explosive device combined with radioactive materials, falling into the hands of terrorists poses a grave threat to national security. The Department of Homeland Security (DHS) has been working tirelessly to counter these threats and safeguard the nation against the making of a dirty bomb.

One of the key vulnerabilities of nuclear systems lies in their increasing reliance on digital systems and networks. As these systems become more interconnected, they become more susceptible to cyberattacks. A successful attack on a nuclear facility's control systems could have devastating consequences, leading to the theft of radioactive materials or even a catastrophic release of radiation.

To address these vulnerabilities, stringent security protocols are required for both nuclear facilities and transportation networks. Regular security audits and risk assessments are crucial in identifying potential weaknesses and implementing necessary security measures.

This includes physical security enhancements, access controls, and surveillance systems to deter and detect unauthorized access.

Furthermore, cybersecurity measures must be implemented to prevent terrorist hacking of nuclear systems. These measures involve robust firewalls, intrusion detection systems, and encryption protocols to secure critical networks and prevent unauthorized access. Regular cybersecurity training for personnel is also essential to ensure awareness of the evolving cyber threat landscape and the adoption of best practices.

Effective radiation detection and monitoring strategies are also vital in mitigating the risk of a dirty bomb incident. The deployment of advanced detection technologies, such as radiation sensors and monitoring systems, can help identify potential threats and provide early warning to security agents. Additionally, intelligence gathering on terrorist organizations' interest in dirty bombs is crucial for proactive prevention.

International cooperation and information sharing play a pivotal role in combating nuclear threats. Close collaboration between countries, intelligence agencies, and law enforcement bodies is essential to exchange information on emerging threats and share best practices. This collective effort enhances the overall security posture and minimizes the chances of successful attacks.

Emergency response plans and preparedness for dirty bomb incidents are equally important. Regular drills and simulations enable security agents to effectively respond to such incidents, minimizing the potential damage and ensuring public safety. Public awareness campaigns are also necessary to educate and inform the general public about the dangers of dirty bombs, encouraging vigilance and reporting any suspicious activities.

To deter individuals involved in dirty bomb activities, robust legal frameworks and penalties must be established. Strict enforcement of laws and severe consequences for those engaged in illicit activities related to dirty bombs serve as a strong deterrent.

Finally, ongoing research and development of advanced technologies are vital to enhance dirty bomb prevention efforts. Investment in cutting-edge technologies, such as artificial intelligence, machine learning, and quantum encryption, can help stay ahead of cyber threats and strengthen the overall resilience of nuclear systems.

In conclusion, the vulnerabilities of nuclear systems to cyberattacks pose a significant threat to national security. The comprehensive implementation of security protocols, cybersecurity measures, radiation detection strategies, intelligence gathering, international cooperation, emergency response plans, public awareness campaigns, legal frameworks, and technological advancements are essential in preventing the making of a dirty bomb. By addressing these vulnerabilities head-on, security agents and the Department of Homeland Security can effectively combat this grave threat and ensure the safety of the nation.

Safeguarding Nuclear Facilities from Cyber Threats

In recent years, the world has witnessed an alarming increase in cyber threats targeting critical infrastructure, including nuclear facilities. The potential consequences of a successful cyber attack on a nuclear facility are devastating, making it essential for security agents to understand and implement effective cybersecurity measures. This subchapter aims to provide crucial insights into safeguarding nuclear facilities from cyber threats, ensuring the safety and security of these vital installations.

The threat of cyber attacks on nuclear facilities has become more sophisticated and prevalent. Terrorist organizations and malicious actors are constantly seeking ways to exploit vulnerabilities in the digital systems that control and monitor nuclear facilities. The consequences of a successful cyber attack on these systems could range from unauthorized access to critical information, tampering with safety protocols, or even the manipulation of nuclear processes, leading to catastrophic outcomes.

To counter these threats, security agents must be well-versed in the latest cybersecurity measures. This includes implementing robust firewalls, intrusion detection systems, and encryption protocols to protect against unauthorized access. Regular vulnerability assessments and penetration testing should be conducted to identify and address any weaknesses in the system.

Furthermore, close coordination and information sharing among national and international agencies are crucial in preventing cyber attacks on nuclear facilities. Intelligence gathering on terrorist organizations' interest in dirty bombs and sharing this information across borders can help identify potential threats before they materialize. International cooperation also plays a significant role in the exchange of best practices and technological advancements to enhance cybersecurity efforts.

In addition to cyber threats, security agents must also focus on radiation detection and monitoring strategies within nuclear facilities. Advanced technologies, such as remote sensing and real-time monitoring systems, can enhance the detection of radiation leaks or unauthorized movement of nuclear materials.

Emergency response plans and preparedness for dirty bomb incidents should be in place to ensure a swift and effective response in case of an attack. Regular drills and training exercises should be conducted to familiarize security agents with the necessary protocols and procedures.

Public awareness campaigns are crucial to educating the general population about the dangers of dirty bombs. By raising public awareness, individuals can become the eyes and ears of law enforcement agencies, reporting any suspicious activities or potential threats.

Lastly, legal frameworks and penalties for individuals involved in dirty bomb activities should be robust and comprehensive. The legal consequences must act as a strong deterrent against engaging in such activities.

In conclusion, safeguarding nuclear facilities from cyber threats requires a multi-faceted approach, with a focus on advanced cybersecurity measures, radiation detection technologies, international cooperation, emergency response plans, public awareness campaigns, and stringent legal frameworks. By implementing these measures, security agents can ensure the safety and security of nuclear facilities, preventing terrorists from acquiring the materials necessary for the making of a dirty bomb.

Collaboration between Cybersecurity Experts and Nuclear Industry

In today's interconnected world, the collaboration between cybersecurity experts and the nuclear industry has become paramount in ensuring the safety and security of our nations. This subchapter delves into the critical partnership between these two entities, highlighting their joint efforts in combating the threat of dirty bombs and safeguarding our homeland.

The Department of Homeland Security, in its relentless pursuit of thwarting terrorist activities, has recognized the need for a strong alliance between cybersecurity experts and the nuclear industry. Cybersecurity measures are now an integral part of nuclear facilities' security protocols, as they are instrumental in preventing terrorist hacking of nuclear systems. With the potential catastrophic consequences of such attacks, it is imperative that the nuclear industry remains at the forefront of cybersecurity advancements.

Nuclear materials detection and tracking technologies have also seen significant developments through collaboration between cybersecurity experts and the nuclear industry. These technologies play a vital role in identifying and monitoring the movement of nuclear materials, making it harder for terrorists to acquire them for the manufacturing of dirty bombs. By leveraging cyber capabilities, experts have enhanced the efficiency and accuracy of these detection systems, minimizing the risk posed by illicit nuclear material transfers.

Intelligence gathering on terrorist organizations' interest in dirty bombs is another area where collaboration has proved invaluable. Through information sharing and international cooperation, cybersecurity experts and the nuclear industry have bolstered their ability to identify and assess potential threats. By staying one step ahead of these terrorist organizations, security agents can better implement preventive measures and neutralize potential threats before they materialize.

Emergency response plans and preparedness for dirty bomb incidents have also benefited greatly from the collaboration between cybersecurity experts and the nuclear industry. By leveraging cyber technologies, experts have developed sophisticated monitoring and radiation detection strategies, ensuring a prompt and effective response in the event of a dirty bomb incident. This collaborative effort has significantly enhanced our emergency response capabilities, minimizing the potential impact of such attacks.

Furthermore, public awareness campaigns on the dangers of dirty bombs have been successful in large part due to the collaboration between these two entities. By combining their expertise, cybersecurity experts and the nuclear industry have effectively conveyed the severity of the threat, ensuring that the public remains informed and vigilant.

In conclusion, the collaboration between cybersecurity experts and the nuclear industry is an essential component in the fight against dirty bombs. Through their combined efforts, security agents can better navigate the challenges posed by terrorism, ensuring the safety and security of our nations. This subchapter highlights the importance of this partnership and serves as a guide for those involved in the making of a dirty bomb and the Department of Homeland Security's efforts to prevent it.

Chapter 5: Radiation Detection and Monitoring Strategies

Technologies for Detecting Radiation

Radiation detection and monitoring strategies play a crucial role in preventing the creation and detonation of dirty bombs. These technologies are essential in safeguarding our nation against the threat of nuclear terrorism. In this subchapter, we will explore the various technologies employed by security agents to detect radiation and protect our homeland.

One of the primary technologies used for detecting radiation is the radiation detection portal monitor. These monitors are installed at key checkpoints such as airports, seaports, and border crossings. They use sophisticated sensors to scan individuals, vehicles, and cargo for the presence of radioactive materials. The portal monitors provide real-time results, enabling security agents to identify and isolate potential threats quickly.

Another critical technology in radiation detection is the handheld radiation detector. These portable devices allow security agents to scan suspicious items or areas for the presence of radioactive materials. Handheld detectors are especially useful in situations where immediate response is required, such as during security sweeps or emergency incidents.

In recent years, advancements in technology have led to the development of more sophisticated radiation detection systems. These include the use of gamma-ray spectrometry, which enables security agents to identify the specific type of radioactive material present. This information is crucial in determining the potential threat level and in devising an appropriate response strategy.

Furthermore, the use of unmanned aerial vehicles (UAVs) equipped with radiation detection sensors has revolutionized radiation monitoring. These UAVs can cover large areas quickly, providing real-time data on radiation levels and hotspots. This technology allows security agents to identify and respond to potential threats more effectively.

To enhance radiation detection capabilities, the Department of Homeland Security has also invested in research and development of advanced technologies. This includes the exploration of artificial intelligence and machine learning algorithms to improve the accuracy and speed of radiation detection systems.

In conclusion, the development and utilization of technologies for detecting radiation play a critical role in our efforts to prevent the creation and detonation of dirty bombs. These technologies, including radiation detection portal monitors, handheld detectors, gamma-ray spectrometry, UAVs, and advanced algorithms, enable security agents to identify and respond to potential threats swiftly and effectively. By staying at the forefront of technological advancements, we can enhance our dirty bomb prevention efforts and ensure the safety and security of our nation.

Monitoring Systems for Radiation Levels

In the fight against the making of a dirty bomb, monitoring systems for radiation levels play a crucial role in safeguarding national security. These systems are designed to detect and track nuclear materials, ensuring their secure transportation and preventing their unauthorized use by terrorists. This subchapter explores the various monitoring technologies and strategies employed by the Department of Homeland Security (DHS) and security agents in their efforts to combat this grave threat.

One of the key components of radiation monitoring systems is the use of advanced detection and tracking technologies. These include gamma-ray spectrometry, neutron detectors, and gamma-ray imaging systems. These state-of-the-art technologies enable security agents to identify and locate potential sources of radiation accurately. Additionally, the DHS has invested in the development of portable radiation detectors, allowing agents to conduct on-site inspections of suspicious objects or individuals.

To enhance the security of nuclear facilities and transportation, stringent security protocols have been put in place. These protocols involve the use of access controls, radiation portal monitors, and vehicle screening systems. By implementing these measures, security agents can detect and deter any illicit attempt to access or transport nuclear materials.

In an increasingly digital world, cybersecurity measures are essential to prevent terrorist hacking of nuclear systems. The DHS has established robust cybersecurity protocols to safeguard critical infrastructure from cyber threats. These measures include network security, encryption, and continuous monitoring of digital systems to detect any suspicious activities.

Intelligence gathering plays a pivotal role in understanding terrorist organizations' interest in dirty bombs. By gathering and analyzing intelligence from various sources, security agents can identify potential threats and take proactive measures to prevent their realization. International cooperation and information sharing are crucial in this regard, as they enable the exchange of intelligence and best practices between nations.

In the event of a dirty bomb incident, emergency response plans and preparedness are vital. These plans involve coordination between law enforcement agencies, first responders, and public health authorities.

Regular drills and exercises are conducted to ensure a seamless response to such incidents, minimizing casualties and containing the spread of radiation.

Public awareness campaigns play a significant role in educating the public about the dangers of dirty bombs. By raising awareness about the potential consequences, individuals are more likely to report suspicious activities and become active partners in national security efforts.

Legal frameworks and penalties are essential to deter individuals involved in dirty bomb activities. Strict laws and severe penalties act as a deterrent, ensuring that those who engage in such activities face the full force of the law.

Finally, ongoing research and development of advanced technologies further enhance dirty bomb prevention efforts. The DHS continually invests in innovative solutions, such as the development of new detection systems and enhanced data analytics, to stay ahead of evolving threats.

In conclusion, monitoring systems for radiation levels form a critical component of the DHS's comprehensive efforts to combat the making of a dirty bomb. By employing advanced technologies, implementing stringent security protocols, and fostering international cooperation, security agents are at the forefront of safeguarding national security and preventing this grave threat.

Importance of Continuous Monitoring in High-Risk Areas

High-risk areas, such as nuclear facilities or transportation routes for nuclear materials, pose a significant threat to national security. The potential for terrorists to acquire and use these materials in the creation of a dirty bomb is a persistent concern for security agents and the

Department of Homeland Security. In order to effectively combat this threat, continuous monitoring of these areas is of utmost importance.

Continuous monitoring provides real-time information on the status and integrity of high-risk areas. It allows security agents to detect any unauthorized access, potential breaches, or suspicious activities that could indicate an impending threat. By constantly monitoring these areas, security agents can quickly respond to any security breaches, preventing terrorists from gaining access to sensitive materials and reducing the risk of a dirty bomb incident.

One key aspect of continuous monitoring is the use of advanced nuclear materials detection and tracking technologies. These technologies help security agents identify any anomalies or irregularities in the movement and storage of nuclear materials. By tracking the movement of these materials, security agents can closely monitor their whereabouts and detect any attempts to divert or steal them.

In addition to nuclear materials detection and tracking technologies, security protocols play a crucial role in ensuring the safety of high-risk areas. These protocols outline the procedures for access control, personnel screening, and security measures to be implemented. Continuous monitoring allows security agents to ensure that these protocols are being followed and to address any deviations or vulnerabilities promptly.

The importance of continuous monitoring extends beyond physical security measures. Cybersecurity measures are equally vital in preventing terrorist hacking of nuclear systems. Continuous monitoring of cyber systems can help identify and mitigate any cybersecurity threats, ensuring that critical infrastructure remains secure from potential attacks.

Radiation detection and monitoring strategies are also essential in high-risk areas. Continuous monitoring of radiation levels helps security agents identify any abnormal radiation signatures that could be indicative of a dirty bomb or illicit nuclear activity. By continuously monitoring radiation levels, security agents can quickly respond to any potential threats and prevent the situation from escalating.

Intelligence gathering on terrorist organizations' interest in dirty bombs is another critical aspect of continuous monitoring. By staying updated on the activities and intentions of these organizations, security agents can anticipate potential threats and take proactive measures to prevent the acquisition or use of nuclear materials for malicious purposes.

International cooperation and information sharing play a vital role in continuous monitoring efforts. Collaboration between different countries allows for the exchange of intelligence, best practices, and technological advancements. By sharing information on nuclear threats, countries can collectively work towards enhancing their monitoring capabilities and preventing the proliferation of dirty bombs.

Emergency response plans and preparedness for dirty bomb incidents are essential components of continuous monitoring efforts. By continuously reviewing and updating these plans, security agents can ensure that they are well-prepared to handle any dirty bomb incidents effectively. Regular drills and simulations help identify any gaps in preparedness and provide valuable insights for improvement.

Public awareness campaigns are also crucial in promoting the importance of continuous monitoring and the dangers of dirty bombs. By educating the public about the risks associated with dirty bombs, individuals can become more vigilant and report any suspicious activities, contributing to the overall security efforts.

Legal frameworks and penalties for individuals involved in dirty bomb activities serve as deterrents and provide a legal basis for prosecuting those involved in illicit nuclear activities. Continuous monitoring helps gather evidence and identify individuals who may be engaged in activities related to dirty bombs, ensuring that they are held accountable for their actions.

Finally, research and development of advanced technologies are essential to enhance dirty bomb prevention efforts. Continuous monitoring allows for the testing and implementation of these advanced technologies, ensuring that security agents have access to the latest tools and techniques to combat the evolving threats.

In conclusion, continuous monitoring is of utmost importance in high-risk areas to prevent the making of a dirty bomb by terrorists. By utilizing advanced technologies, implementing strict security protocols, monitoring cyber systems, detecting radiation levels, gathering intelligence, promoting international cooperation, and ensuring emergency preparedness, security agents can effectively mitigate the risks associated with dirty bombs. Through public awareness campaigns, legal frameworks, and continuous research and development, we can enhance our prevention efforts and safeguard national security against this grave threat.

Chapter 6: Intelligence Gathering on Terrorist Organizations' Interest in Dirty Bombs

Role of Intelligence Agencies in Identifying Threats

The Role of Intelligence Agencies in Identifying Threats

In the fight against the making of a dirty bomb and to ensure the safety of our homeland, the role of intelligence agencies is paramount. These agencies play a crucial role in identifying threats and gathering vital information to prevent any potential attacks. This subchapter explores the various ways intelligence agencies contribute to this effort.

One of the key responsibilities of intelligence agencies is gathering intelligence on terrorist organizations' interest in dirty bombs. Through extensive surveillance, infiltrating terrorist networks, and monitoring online activities, these agencies are able to identify potential threats and their intentions. By staying ahead of the game, they can provide valuable information to other security agents and help prevent any attempts at building a dirty bomb.

International cooperation and information sharing are also critical in combating the threat of dirty bombs. Intelligence agencies work closely with their counterparts in other countries to share intelligence and exchange information on nuclear threats. This collaboration allows for a more comprehensive understanding of the global threat landscape and enhances our ability to prevent any potential attacks.

Intelligence agencies also contribute to the development of advanced technologies and research aimed at enhancing dirty bomb prevention efforts. By investing in research and development, these agencies ensure that we stay ahead of the ever-evolving threat landscape. From nuclear materials detection and tracking technologies to cybersecurity measures and radiation detection strategies, intelligence agencies play a crucial role in driving innovation in these areas.

Additionally, intelligence agencies are instrumental in the formulation of emergency response plans and preparedness for dirty bomb incidents. By analyzing potential scenarios and collecting intelligence on potential targets, they help shape effective emergency response strategies. This ensures that in the event of an attack, the response is swift and effective, minimizing the potential damage and loss of life.

Public awareness campaigns on the dangers of dirty bombs are another area where intelligence agencies contribute significantly. By disseminating information to the public, they raise awareness about the threat and empower individuals to be vigilant. This collective effort is essential in preventing attacks and ensuring the safety of our communities.

Lastly, intelligence agencies play a vital role in establishing legal frameworks and penalties for individuals involved in dirty bomb activities. By working closely with lawmakers, they help shape legislation that holds individuals accountable for their actions. This acts as a deterrent and strengthens our ability to prosecute those involved in the making of a dirty bomb.

In conclusion, intelligence agencies are at the forefront of identifying threats and preventing the making of a dirty bomb. Through their intelligence gathering, international cooperation, research and development, emergency preparedness efforts, public awareness campaigns, and legal frameworks, they play a crucial role in safeguarding our nation. Their efforts are essential in the ongoing fight against terrorism and ensuring the safety and security of our homeland.

Methods of Collecting Information on Terrorist Activities

In the ongoing battle against terrorism, it is imperative for security agents to stay one step ahead of the ever-evolving tactics used by these dangerous groups. Collecting accurate and timely information on terrorist activities is crucial to prevent catastrophic incidents, such as the making of a dirty bomb. This subchapter explores various methods that can be employed to gather valuable intelligence on terrorist organizations' interest in dirty bombs, ensuring the safety and security of the nation.

One of the key methods is intelligence gathering through human sources. Security agents rely on informants, undercover agents, and confidential sources who infiltrate terrorist organizations and provide valuable insights into their activities. These individuals play a critical role in identifying potential threats and gathering information on their plans to acquire or construct a dirty bomb.

Additionally, technological advancements have significantly enhanced the collection of information on terrorist activities. Surveillance systems, satellite imagery, and drones equipped with advanced sensors can be utilized to monitor suspicious activities and locations. These technologies aid in tracking the movement of individuals, identifying potential nuclear materials smuggling routes, and detecting any illicit activities related to dirty bomb production.

Furthermore, cybersecurity measures are essential to prevent terrorist hacking of nuclear systems. As terrorists become more technologically sophisticated, it is crucial to protect nuclear facilities' computer networks from cyber-attacks. Robust cybersecurity protocols, such as firewalls, encryption, and frequent system updates, ensure the integrity and confidentiality of sensitive information.

International cooperation and information sharing play a vital role in combating nuclear threats. Security agents must collaborate with intelligence agencies and law enforcement organizations worldwide to exchange information on potential terrorist activities. These partnerships facilitate the identification of global networks involved in the production and trafficking of nuclear materials.

Emergency response plans and preparedness are equally important aspects of preventing dirty bomb incidents. Security agents must develop comprehensive strategies to effectively respond to and mitigate the consequences of a dirty bomb attack. Regular drills and simulations help refine these plans, ensuring a coordinated and swift response in the event of an incident.

Public awareness campaigns are also crucial in educating the general public about the dangers of dirty bombs. By raising awareness and promoting a culture of vigilance, citizens become active participants in preventing terrorist activities and reporting suspicious behaviors.

Finally, legal frameworks and penalties for individuals involved in dirty bomb activities serve as strong deterrents. Strict laws and severe punishments act as a deterrent to potential terrorists, making it significantly harder for them to carry out their malicious plans.

To stay ahead of terrorists, continuous research and development of advanced technologies is imperative. These efforts aim to enhance dirty bomb prevention, detection, and mitigation strategies. By investing in cutting-edge technologies, security agents can adapt to the ever-changing threat landscape and effectively safeguard the nation against potential dirty bomb attacks.

In conclusion, the methods of collecting information on terrorist activities are diverse and multifaceted. From human intelligence sources to advanced surveillance systems, each method plays a critical role in preventing the making of a dirty bomb. The combination of these strategies, along with international cooperation, public awareness campaigns, and stringent legal frameworks, ensures the effective protection of nuclear facilities and the safety of the nation.

Analyzing and Assessing Terrorist Intentions and Capabilities

In the subchapter "Analyzing and Assessing Terrorist Intentions and Capabilities" of the book "Inside the Threat: The Making of a Dirty Bomb and Homeland Security's Fight to Stop It," we delve into the crucial task of understanding the motivations and capabilities of terrorists who seek to create a dirty bomb. This subchapter is specifically tailored to the knowledge needs of security agents who play a vital role in safeguarding our nation against this grave threat.

To effectively combat the making of a dirty bomb, security agents must possess a deep understanding of the entire process, from the acquisition of nuclear materials to the assembly and deployment of the bomb. This subchapter provides an in-depth examination of various aspects related to this threat, including nuclear materials detection and tracking technologies, security protocols for nuclear facilities and transportation, and cybersecurity measures to prevent terrorist hacking of nuclear systems.

Furthermore, intelligence gathering on terrorist organizations' interest in dirty bombs is crucial for identifying potential threats before they materialize. This subchapter explores the methodologies and strategies employed by security agencies to gather actionable intelligence on terrorist intentions and capabilities, enabling proactive measures to disrupt their plans.

International cooperation and information sharing play a vital role in combating the threat of dirty bombs. This subchapter emphasizes the importance of collaboration between nations, sharing intelligence, best practices, and technological advancements to enhance our collective ability to prevent and respond to nuclear threats.

Emergency response plans and preparedness for dirty bomb incidents are crucial components of a comprehensive security strategy. This subchapter provides insights into the development of effective emergency response plans, training protocols, and coordination mechanisms, ensuring a rapid and efficient response in the event of a dirty bomb incident.

To bolster our defense against dirty bombs, public awareness campaigns are essential. This subchapter explores the significance of educating the public about the dangers associated with dirty bombs, fostering a sense of collective responsibility and vigilance among citizens.

Lastly, legal frameworks and penalties play a pivotal role in deterring individuals involved in dirty bomb activities. This subchapter delves into the existing legal frameworks, highlighting the importance of strict penalties for those engaged in the creation, possession, or use of dirty bombs.

As the threat of dirty bombs continues to evolve, research and development of advanced technologies become paramount. This subchapter highlights ongoing efforts to develop innovative and cutting-edge technologies that enhance our ability to prevent, detect, and respond to the making of dirty bombs.

By delving into these crucial topics, this subchapter equips security agents with the necessary knowledge to effectively analyze and assess terrorist intentions and capabilities regarding the creation of dirty bombs. With this enhanced understanding, security agents can play a pivotal role in safeguarding our nation and countering this significant threat to our security and well-being.

Chapter 7: International Cooperation and Information Sharing on Nuclear Threats

Collaborative Efforts between Countries on Nuclear Security

In the fight against the threat of dirty bombs, collaboration between countries plays a vital role in safeguarding global security. The international community recognizes the urgency and seriousness of this threat, and concerted efforts are being made to prevent terrorists from acquiring and using nuclear materials. This subchapter explores the collaborative initiatives between countries on nuclear security and highlights the various strategies employed to counter this threat.

One of the most critical aspects of collaborative efforts is the sharing of information and intelligence on nuclear threats. Countries are actively engaged in gathering and analyzing intelligence on terrorist organizations' interest in dirty bombs. Through international cooperation, security agents from different nations exchange valuable information, enabling a comprehensive understanding of the evolving threat landscape. This collective intelligence helps in identifying potential targets, tracking suspicious activities, and apprehending individuals involved in dirty bomb activities.

Additionally, countries are working together to enhance the detection and tracking of nuclear materials. Advanced technologies, such as nuclear materials detection and tracking technologies, are being developed through collaborative research and development programs. These technologies enable security agents to identify and locate nuclear materials, both within and outside of nuclear facilities. Furthermore, international cooperation ensures the implementation of robust security protocols for the transportation of nuclear materials, reducing the risk of theft or diversion.

Cybersecurity measures are also a crucial component of collaborative efforts. Countries are sharing best practices and intelligence on preventing terrorist hacking of nuclear systems. By collectively strengthening their cybersecurity infrastructure, nations can minimize the vulnerability of nuclear facilities to cyber-attacks, ensuring that critical systems remain protected.

In addition to prevention, countries are actively engaged in developing emergency response plans and preparedness for dirty bomb incidents. Collaborative efforts enable the sharing of expertise and best practices in handling and mitigating the consequences of a dirty bomb detonation. Through joint training exercises and simulations, security agents gain valuable experience in responding to such incidents, thereby enhancing the overall preparedness and resilience of nations.

Public awareness campaigns also form an integral part of collaborative efforts. By disseminating information on the dangers of dirty bombs to the general public, countries aim to raise awareness and promote vigilance. This collective effort helps in creating a sense of shared responsibility, empowering citizens to report suspicious activities and contribute to overall security.

Lastly, collaborative efforts extend to the development of legal frameworks and penalties for individuals involved in dirty bomb activities. Countries are working together to establish stringent laws and regulations to deter and punish those engaged in the production or use of dirty bombs. By aligning their legal systems, nations can effectively prosecute offenders and dismantle terrorist networks involved in the dirty bomb trade.

In conclusion, collaborative efforts between countries on nuclear security are crucial in preventing the making and usage of dirty bombs by terrorists. Through international cooperation, countries are strengthening their intelligence gathering, enhancing detection technologies, fortifying cybersecurity measures, developing emergency response plans, raising public awareness, and enforcing legal frameworks. By working together, security agents from different nations can effectively combat the threat of dirty bombs and safeguard global security.

Sharing Intelligence and Best Practices

In the fight against the making of a dirty bomb, intelligence gathering and sharing best practices are critical components of Homeland Security's efforts. This subchapter delves into the importance of collaboration, information sharing, and the exchange of best practices among security agents to prevent the creation of a dirty bomb.

The Department of Homeland Security recognizes the gravity of the threat posed by terrorists seeking to obtain and use nuclear materials for malicious purposes. To counter this threat effectively, it is essential for security agents to share intelligence on the tactics, techniques, and procedures employed by these dangerous individuals or organizations.

Sharing intelligence allows security agents to stay one step ahead of potential threats and adapt their strategies accordingly. This includes sharing information on terrorist organizations' interest in dirty bombs, their recruitment methods, and their supply chain networks. By pooling resources and sharing information, security agencies can identify patterns, track potential suspects, and disrupt their operations before they can carry out any attacks.

Furthermore, sharing best practices among security agents is crucial for enhancing security protocols at nuclear facilities and during transportation. It involves the exchange of knowledge on the latest nuclear materials detection and tracking technologies, cybersecurity measures to prevent terrorist hacking of nuclear systems, and radiation detection and monitoring strategies. This collaboration ensures that security measures remain up-to-date and incorporate the latest advancements in technology.

International cooperation is also emphasized in this subchapter. Given the global nature of the threat, it is imperative for security agents worldwide to work together, sharing information and coordinating efforts to combat the making of dirty bombs. This includes establishing channels for information sharing, conducting joint training exercises, and fostering partnerships between countries to enhance overall security.

Emergency response plans and preparedness for dirty bomb incidents are also discussed in this subchapter. Security agents need to be well-prepared to respond swiftly and effectively in the event of a dirty bomb incident. Sharing best practices in emergency response planning and conducting realistic drills can ensure a coordinated and efficient response, minimizing the impact of such an attack.

Public awareness campaigns play a vital role in preventing the making of dirty bombs. Security agents must educate the public about the dangers posed by these weapons and the importance of reporting suspicious activities. This subchapter explores various approaches to raise public awareness and foster a sense of responsibility and vigilance within communities.

Finally, this subchapter addresses the legal frameworks and penalties for individuals involved in dirty bomb activities. By understanding the legal consequences and working within the established frameworks, security agents can ensure that those responsible for planning and executing dirty bomb attacks are held accountable for their actions.

To stay ahead of evolving threats, research and development of advanced technologies are critical. This subchapter explores ongoing efforts to develop innovative technologies that can enhance dirty bomb prevention efforts, such as improved detection systems, advanced surveillance tools, and cutting-edge radiation monitoring devices.

In conclusion, sharing intelligence and best practices is essential in the fight against the making of a dirty bomb. By collaborating, exchanging information, and implementing the most effective strategies, security agents can enhance their capabilities and prevent terrorists from obtaining and using nuclear materials for destructive purposes. This subchapter provides valuable insights and guidance for security agents striving to protect their nations and secure a safer future.

Challenges and Benefits of International Cooperation

In the face of the ever-evolving threat landscape, international cooperation has become increasingly crucial in combating the proliferation of dirty bombs and safeguarding national security. This subchapter explores the challenges and benefits associated with international cooperation in the fight against nuclear terrorism.

One of the primary challenges is the coordination of efforts among different countries with varying priorities and capabilities. Each nation has unique concerns and resources, making it difficult to establish a unified approach. However, the benefits of international cooperation are manifold. By pooling resources, intelligence, and expertise, security agents can enhance their ability to detect, prevent, and respond to threats effectively.

International cooperation fosters the sharing of vital information on nuclear threats. Through robust intelligence gathering, security agencies can identify terrorist organizations' interest in dirty bombs and their plans for acquisition or production. By collaborating and sharing this intelligence, countries can collectively strengthen their defenses and develop targeted strategies to counter the specific threats posed by these organizations.

Another significant benefit of international cooperation is the establishment of comprehensive security protocols for nuclear facilities and transportation. By sharing best practices and lessons learned, security agents can develop more effective methods to detect, track, and secure nuclear materials. This collaborative approach ensures that security measures are implemented consistently across borders, limiting potential vulnerabilities that terrorists could exploit.

Cybersecurity measures are also a critical aspect of international cooperation in preventing terrorist hacking of nuclear systems. By sharing expertise and intelligence on cyber threats, countries can collectively develop robust defense mechanisms and protocols to safeguard nuclear infrastructure from cyber attacks.

Furthermore, international cooperation enables the exchange of radiation detection and monitoring strategies. By sharing research, technological advancements, and best practices, security agents can enhance their capabilities in detecting and responding to radiological threats promptly. This collaboration ensures that countries worldwide are equipped with the latest tools and knowledge to mitigate the risks associated with dirty bombs.

Emergency response plans and preparedness for dirty bomb incidents are also strengthened through international cooperation. By sharing experiences and resources, security agencies can develop comprehensive and coordinated response strategies. This collaboration ensures a swift and effective response in the event of a dirty bomb incident, minimizing the potential damage and impact on public safety.

In addition to these practical benefits, international cooperation also allows for the development of legal frameworks and penalties for individuals involved in dirty bomb activities. By aligning legal systems and penalties across borders, nations can ensure that terrorists and their accomplices face severe consequences for their actions, deterring potential threats.

Lastly, international cooperation facilitates research and development of advanced technologies to enhance dirty bomb prevention efforts. By pooling resources and expertise, countries can accelerate the development of innovative technologies that improve detection, tracking, and prevention capabilities.

In conclusion, the challenges of international cooperation in the fight against nuclear terrorism are significant, but the benefits outweigh them. Through collaboration, security agents can enhance their ability to detect, prevent, and respond to dirty bomb threats effectively. By sharing intelligence, best practices, and resources, nations can collectively strengthen their defenses, develop comprehensive security protocols, improve emergency response plans, and deter potential threats. International cooperation is an essential tool in the fight against nuclear terrorism, ensuring the safety and security of nations worldwide.

Chapter 8: Emergency Response Plans and Preparedness for Dirty Bomb Incidents

Developing Effective Emergency Response Plans

Emergency response plans are crucial in ensuring the preparedness and effectiveness of security agents in dealing with the threat of dirty bombs. In this subchapter, we will explore the key elements involved in developing such plans and the importance of coordination and cooperation among various stakeholders.

First and foremost, emergency response plans should be tailored to the specific needs and vulnerabilities of each location or nuclear facility. This requires a thorough understanding of the potential risks and the impact that a dirty bomb incident could have on the surrounding areas. Security agents must work closely with experts in nuclear materials detection and tracking technologies to assess the potential threats and develop strategies to mitigate them.

Effective security protocols for nuclear facilities and transportation are also essential in preventing terrorists from gaining access to radioactive materials. These protocols should include stringent access control measures, regular inspections, and the use of advanced technologies for detecting and preventing unauthorized entry. Additionally, cybersecurity measures must be in place to prevent terrorist hacking of nuclear systems, which could lead to the theft or sabotage of radioactive materials.

Radiation detection and monitoring strategies play a crucial role in identifying the presence of a dirty bomb and assessing the extent of the contamination. Security agents should be equipped with state-of-the-art detection devices and trained to quickly and accurately interpret the results. Regular drills and exercises should be conducted to ensure the readiness of security personnel in responding to such incidents.

Intelligence gathering on terrorist organizations' interest in dirty bombs is vital in preventing their development and use. Close collaboration with intelligence agencies and international partners is necessary to share information and stay ahead of evolving threats. International cooperation and information sharing on nuclear threats are essential in addressing the global nature of this issue and ensuring a coordinated response.

Emergency response plans should also include strategies for public awareness campaigns on the dangers of dirty bombs. Educating the public about the risks and promoting vigilance can help in preventing attacks and minimizing panic in the event of an incident.

Furthermore, legal frameworks and penalties for individuals involved in dirty bomb activities need to be in place to deter potential perpetrators. Strict enforcement of these laws will help to disrupt terrorist networks and hold those responsible accountable.

Finally, continuous research and development of advanced technologies are essential in enhancing dirty bomb prevention efforts. Investing in innovative solutions for nuclear security will enable security agents to stay ahead of terrorists and effectively mitigate the threats they pose.

In conclusion, developing effective emergency response plans is crucial in addressing the threat of dirty bombs. By focusing on nuclear materials detection and tracking technologies, security protocols, cybersecurity measures, radiation detection and monitoring strategies, intelligence gathering, international cooperation, public awareness campaigns, legal frameworks, and research and development, security agents can significantly enhance their preparedness and response capabilities in preventing and mitigating dirty bomb incidents.

Coordination between Law Enforcement and Emergency Services

In the fight against the threat of a dirty bomb, coordination between law enforcement and emergency services plays a pivotal role. The seamless integration of these two entities is crucial for effective prevention, response, and mitigation efforts. This subchapter explores the significance of this coordination and the strategies employed to ensure a robust security framework.

Law enforcement agencies and emergency services possess distinct yet complementary roles in responding to a dirty bomb incident. While law enforcement focuses on investigation, intelligence gathering, and apprehending the perpetrators, emergency services are responsible for managing the immediate aftermath, including medical response, evacuations, and containment of radiation.

To facilitate coordination, collaborative frameworks and information-sharing protocols must be established. The Department of Homeland Security (DHS) has played a pivotal role in fostering such cooperation through various initiatives. These efforts include joint training exercises, task forces, and fusion centers, where law enforcement and emergency responders can share intelligence, strategies, and best practices.

Another critical aspect of coordination is the development of comprehensive emergency response plans. These plans outline the roles and responsibilities of both law enforcement and emergency services in the event of a dirty bomb incident. Regular drills and exercises should be conducted to test the effectiveness of these plans and identify areas for improvement.

Furthermore, coordination efforts must extend beyond national borders. The international community must work together to combat the threat of dirty bombs, sharing intelligence on terrorist organizations' interest in such weapons and collaborating on prevention and response strategies. International partnerships can enhance the ability to track and intercept illicit nuclear materials, ensuring a global effort to prevent the making of dirty bombs.

Public awareness campaigns are also essential to enlist the support of the general population in identifying and reporting suspicious activities. By educating the public about the dangers of dirty bombs and the importance of reporting any potential threats, law enforcement and emergency services can benefit from the extra eyes and ears of the community.

Finally, legal frameworks and penalties must be in place to deter and punish individuals involved in dirty bomb activities. Strict laws and severe punishments serve as a deterrent and reinforce the seriousness of engaging in such malicious acts.

In conclusion, coordination between law enforcement and emergency services is vital in combating the threat of dirty bombs. Through collaborative frameworks, comprehensive emergency response plans, international cooperation, public awareness campaigns, and robust legal frameworks, security agents can work together to prevent the making of dirty bombs and enhance overall homeland security. Continuous research and development of advanced technologies further strengthen prevention efforts, providing security agents with the tools they need to stay one step ahead of potential threats.

Training and Drills to Enhance Preparedness

In the ever-evolving landscape of global security threats, it is crucial for security agents to be prepared for any potential danger. This subchapter explores the various training and drills that can help enhance preparedness in the face of the potential making of a dirty bomb and the Department of Homeland Security's efforts to stop it. These training programs are designed to equip security agents with the necessary skills and knowledge to effectively counteract the threats posed by terrorists seeking to create a dirty bomb.

One of the key components of training and drills is the use of realistic scenarios. By simulating potential dirty bomb incidents, security agents can gain firsthand experience in handling such situations. These drills involve the coordination of multiple agencies, such as law enforcement, emergency response teams, and nuclear facility personnel, to ensure a seamless and effective response in the event of an actual incident.

Furthermore, training programs focus on the utilization of nuclear materials detection and tracking technologies. Security agents are trained on the latest advancements in this field to ensure the timely identification and interception of any suspicious materials. Additionally, protocols for securing nuclear facilities and transportation are emphasized to prevent unauthorized access and ensure the safe handling of nuclear materials.

In today's digital age, cybersecurity measures play a crucial role in preventing terrorist hacking of nuclear systems. Training programs equip security agents with the necessary skills to identify and thwart cyber threats, ensuring the integrity and confidentiality of nuclear systems.

Radiation detection and monitoring strategies are also an integral part of training and drills. Security agents are trained on the proper use of radiation detection equipment, enabling them to swiftly identify and respond to any potential radiological threats.

Intelligence gathering on terrorist organizations' interest in dirty bombs is another vital aspect of training. Security agents are briefed on the latest intelligence reports and techniques for gathering information on potential threats. International cooperation and information sharing on nuclear threats is also emphasized to ensure a coordinated global response.

Emergency response plans and preparedness for dirty bomb incidents are extensively covered in training programs. Security agents are trained on the proper protocols and procedures to minimize casualties and contain the impact of a dirty bomb detonation. Public awareness campaigns are also undertaken to educate the general public on the dangers of dirty bombs and how to respond in the event of an incident.

Legal frameworks and penalties for individuals involved in dirty bomb activities are highlighted to deter potential perpetrators. Finally, research and development of advanced technologies to enhance dirty bomb prevention efforts are ongoing, and security agents are updated on the latest advancements in this field.

In conclusion, training and drills play a vital role in enhancing preparedness for the making of a dirty bomb and the Department of Homeland Security's efforts to prevent it. By equipping security agents with the necessary skills, knowledge, and technologies, we can ensure a robust response to this grave threat and safeguard the lives and security of our nation and its citizens.

Chapter 9: Public Awareness Campaigns on the Dangers of Dirty Bombs

Importance of Public Awareness in Counterterrorism

The importance of public awareness in counterterrorism cannot be overstated. In the fight against terrorism, it is crucial to involve the general public and raise awareness about the threats posed by dirty bombs. This subchapter delves into the significance of public awareness campaigns and their role in preventing the making of a dirty bomb, as well as the efforts made by the Department of Homeland Security (DHS) in this regard.

Public awareness campaigns are instrumental in educating the masses about the dangers of dirty bombs. By disseminating information about the devastating consequences of these weapons, the public can better understand the urgency of counterterrorism measures. Security agents play a vital role in implementing these campaigns, as they are on the front lines of defense and can effectively communicate the risks associated with dirty bombs.

The DHS has been at the forefront of such awareness initiatives, working tirelessly to engage both the public and relevant stakeholders. Through media campaigns, public service announcements, and outreach programs, the DHS aims to empower individuals with knowledge about the threat landscape and the necessary measures to thwart terrorist activities. By fostering a sense of responsibility and vigilance among the public, the DHS endeavors to create a proactive environment that hinders the making of a dirty bomb.

Moreover, public awareness campaigns also serve to garner support for the security protocols in place for nuclear facilities and transportation. By highlighting the stringent measures taken to safeguard nuclear materials, these campaigns alleviate concerns and build trust in the system. This, in turn, encourages public cooperation and reporting of suspicious activities, leading to enhanced security and prevention of dirty bomb incidents.

In addition, public awareness campaigns foster a culture of resilience and preparedness. By educating individuals on emergency response plans and procedures, the public can actively participate in mitigating the consequences of a dirty bomb incident. Awareness about radiation detection and monitoring strategies equips individuals to safeguard themselves and others in the event of an attack.

To ensure the success of public awareness campaigns, international cooperation and information sharing are imperative. The exchange of knowledge, best practices, and intelligence on nuclear threats between countries facilitates a comprehensive and unified approach to counterterrorism. Collaboration with international partners strengthens public awareness efforts and enhances the global fight against dirty bomb proliferation.

In conclusion, public awareness plays a critical role in counterterrorism efforts, specifically in preventing the making of a dirty bomb. By engaging security agents and the public, the DHS and other relevant authorities can effectively educate individuals about the dangers of these weapons, encourage cooperation, and build a resilient society. Through international cooperation, information sharing, and the development of advanced technologies, the fight against dirty bombs can be intensified, ensuring the safety and security of nations worldwide.

Strategies for Educating the Public about Dirty Bombs

The threat of dirty bombs is a growing concern in today's world, and it is crucial that the public is well-informed about the dangers they pose. In this subchapter, we will explore various strategies for educating the public about dirty bombs and their potential consequences. By disseminating knowledge and raising awareness, we can empower individuals to play an active role in preventing such acts of terrorism.

1. Public Awareness Campaigns: Developing and implementing comprehensive public awareness campaigns is essential. These campaigns should focus on educating the general public about the nature of dirty bombs, their potential impact on human health and the environment, and the importance of reporting any suspicious activities.

2. Collaborative Efforts: Collaboration between government agencies, law enforcement, and private organizations is crucial. By working together, we can pool resources and expertise to create targeted educational programs that effectively reach the public.

3. Use of Various Communication Channels: Utilize a range of communication channels to reach a diverse audience. This includes traditional media outlets such as television, radio, and newspapers, as well as digital platforms like social media, websites, and mobile applications.

4. Engage Community Leaders: Engaging community leaders and influential individuals can help in disseminating information effectively. By collaborating with religious leaders, community organizations, and local influencers, we can reach a broader audience and encourage them to spread the message within their respective communities.

5. School Programs: Integrate education about dirty bombs into school curricula. This will ensure that young people are educated about the threat and understand the importance of reporting any suspicious activities.

6. Public Events and Workshops: Organize public events, workshops, and seminars to provide an opportunity for experts to share information on dirty bombs with the public. These events can also facilitate open discussions and address any concerns or misconceptions.

7. Public-Private Partnerships: Foster collaborations with private organizations, such as media outlets and technology companies, to amplify the reach of educational campaigns. This can involve the creation of public service announcements, articles, and online resources.

8. Crisis Communication Plans: Develop comprehensive crisis communication plans that provide clear and concise information to the public in the event of a dirty bomb incident. This includes guidance on evacuation procedures, sheltering in place, and other necessary safety measures.

9. Continuous Updates: Regularly update educational materials and campaigns to reflect the latest information and developments in the field. This ensures that the public remains well-informed and aware of any emerging threats.

Educating the public about dirty bombs is a shared responsibility. By employing these strategies, we can enhance public awareness, encourage reporting of suspicious activities, and ultimately contribute to the prevention of dirty bomb incidents. Continued efforts in education, collaboration, and communication are vital in our collective fight against this threat to national security.

Engaging Communities in Reporting Suspicious Activities

In the fight against the making of a dirty bomb, it is crucial to engage communities in reporting suspicious activities. Security agents play a vital role in this process, as they are at the forefront of identifying potential threats and safeguarding our nation's security. By encouraging community involvement and awareness, we can strengthen our defenses and prevent catastrophic events.

One of the primary challenges in preventing the making of a dirty bomb is the ability to gather timely and accurate intelligence. Security agents cannot be everywhere at once, which is why community engagement becomes essential. By fostering a culture of reporting suspicious activities, we create an extensive network of eyes and ears that can help identify potential threats.

To achieve this, security agents must build trust and establish strong relationships with communities. Regular outreach programs, public forums, and educational campaigns can be effective tools in raising awareness about the dangers of dirty bombs and the importance of reporting suspicious activities. By openly discussing these issues, we can empower individuals to become active participants in maintaining national security.

In addition to awareness campaigns, leveraging technology can greatly enhance community engagement. Mobile applications, dedicated hotlines, and online reporting platforms can provide a convenient and confidential way for individuals to share their concerns. Anonymity should be emphasized to encourage people who fear retaliation or backlash.

Once reports are received, it is essential to have a robust system in place to evaluate and investigate each case promptly. Security agents should collaborate with local law enforcement agencies and intelligence organizations to ensure a coordinated response. Regular training sessions can also be conducted to educate security agents on the indicators of suspicious activities and the appropriate protocols to follow.

Engaging communities in reporting suspicious activities is not only about prevention but also about building resilience. By involving the public in the fight against dirty bombs, we create a sense of ownership and shared responsibility. This collective effort will enable security agents to gather critical information, respond swiftly to potential threats, and ultimately, deter terrorists from pursuing their sinister goals.

In conclusion, engaging communities in reporting suspicious activities is a crucial aspect of preventing the making of a dirty bomb. By fostering trust, raising awareness, and leveraging technology, security agents can tap into the collective knowledge and vigilance of the public. This collaboration will strengthen our nation's security and ensure the safety of our communities.

Chapter 10: Legal Frameworks and Penalties for Individuals Involved in Dirty Bomb Activities

Legislative Measures to Combat Dirty Bomb Threats

The threat of a dirty bomb, a conventional explosive combined with radioactive material, poses a significant danger to national security and public safety. In response, legislative measures have been enacted to combat and prevent such threats. This subchapter explores the various legislative measures implemented to safeguard against dirty bomb incidents and protect the public from potential harm.

One key legislative measure is the establishment of comprehensive security protocols for nuclear facilities and transportation. These protocols ensure that proper security measures are in place at all stages of the nuclear fuel cycle, from production to disposal. They also require stringent background checks and training for personnel working in these facilities, reducing the risk of insider threats.

Furthermore, cybersecurity measures have been implemented to prevent terrorist hacking of nuclear systems. The Department of Homeland Security has collaborated with various agencies and organizations to develop robust cybersecurity strategies, including advanced encryption methods and intrusion detection systems. These measures aim to protect critical nuclear infrastructure from cyberattacks and unauthorized access.

In addition, legislative efforts have focused on enhancing radiation detection and monitoring strategies. This includes the deployment of advanced detection technologies at ports, borders, and other high-risk areas. These measures aim to identify and intercept any illicit trafficking of radioactive materials, providing an early warning system against potential dirty bomb threats.

Intelligence gathering on terrorist organizations' interest in dirty bombs plays a crucial role in prevention efforts. Legislation has been enacted to enhance information sharing and international cooperation in this regard. Intelligence agencies collaborate with their counterparts worldwide to gather and analyze intelligence on terrorist activities, ensuring early detection of any potential threats involving dirty bombs.

Emergency response plans and preparedness for dirty bomb incidents are also integral to combating this threat. Legislation mandates the development and regular updating of comprehensive response plans at the national, state, and local levels. These plans outline specific procedures for emergency response, evacuation, and decontamination, ensuring a coordinated and effective response in the event of a dirty bomb incident.

Public awareness campaigns on the dangers of dirty bombs have been instrumental in promoting vigilance and encouraging public cooperation. Legislation supports the development of educational materials and outreach programs to inform the public about the potential consequences of a dirty bomb attack. This heightens public awareness and encourages the reporting of suspicious activities or materials.

Finally, legal frameworks and penalties have been established for individuals involved in dirty bomb activities. Legislation ensures that those who engage in the production, acquisition, or use of a dirty bomb face severe legal consequences. These penalties act as a deterrent and provide law enforcement agencies with the necessary tools to prosecute those involved in these activities effectively.

To further strengthen prevention efforts, ongoing research and development of advanced technologies are being pursued. Legislation supports research initiatives aimed at enhancing dirty bomb prevention, detection, and response capabilities. This includes the development of innovative technologies, such as improved radiation detection devices, advanced modeling and simulation tools, and more effective decontamination methods.

In conclusion, legislative measures play a vital role in combating the threat of dirty bombs. Through the establishment of security protocols, cybersecurity measures, radiation detection strategies, intelligence gathering, international cooperation, emergency response plans, public awareness campaigns, legal frameworks, and research and development efforts, security agents can work together to prevent and mitigate the risks associated with dirty bomb incidents. These legislative measures reinforce the Department of Homeland Security's commitment to ensuring the safety and security of the nation and its citizens.

Prosecution and Sentencing of Individuals Involved in Dirty Bomb Activities

In the fight against the looming threat of dirty bombs, the prosecution and sentencing of individuals involved in such activities become vital components of our security efforts. This subchapter delves into the legal frameworks and penalties put in place to ensure that those responsible for these heinous acts are held accountable for their actions.

The Department of Homeland Security, in collaboration with various law enforcement agencies, has taken significant steps to develop comprehensive legal strategies to combat the production and use of dirty bombs. Prosecution of individuals involved in these activities is a crucial aspect of these strategies, aimed at deterring potential perpetrators and ensuring justice is served.

To effectively prosecute and sentence individuals involved in dirty bomb activities, it is imperative to have a robust legal framework in place. This framework includes stringent laws that classify dirty bomb activities as severe offenses, punishable by severe penalties. These penalties may range from lengthy imprisonment to significant fines, depending on the severity of the offense and the intent of the individual involved.

Additionally, the legal framework encompasses provisions for investigating and gathering evidence against individuals suspected of dirty bomb activities. This involves utilizing advanced technologies and intelligence gathering techniques to track and gather substantial evidence to support the prosecution's case.

Furthermore, international cooperation and information sharing play a crucial role in the successful prosecution and sentencing of individuals involved in dirty bomb activities. Through collaboration with other nations, law enforcement agencies can exchange intelligence, share best practices, and enhance their capabilities to identify and apprehend those involved in the production or use of dirty bombs.

The subchapter also highlights the importance of public awareness campaigns on the dangers of dirty bombs. By educating the public, security agents can gather valuable information and gain the support of citizens in reporting suspicious activities, thereby aiding in the prosecution of individuals involved in such activities.

In conclusion, the prosecution and sentencing of individuals involved in dirty bomb activities form a critical part of our comprehensive security efforts. By implementing stringent legal frameworks, collaborating internationally, and raising public awareness, security agents can effectively deter potential perpetrators, gather evidence, and ensure that justice is served. It is through these collective efforts that we can safeguard our nation and protect it from the catastrophic consequences of dirty bombs.

International Efforts to Strengthen Legal Frameworks

In the global fight against terrorism and the proliferation of nuclear materials, international cooperation and the strengthening of legal frameworks play a crucial role. Recognizing the gravity of the threat posed by the making of dirty bombs, efforts have been made to enhance existing legal frameworks and establish new ones to combat this menace. This subchapter explores the international efforts undertaken to strengthen legal frameworks and prevent the making of dirty bombs.

International cooperation and information sharing have become vital components of countering the dirty bomb threat. Various organizations, such as the International Atomic Energy Agency (IAEA) and Interpol, have been actively involved in facilitating information exchange among nations. These platforms enable security agents to gather intelligence on terrorist organizations' interest in dirty bombs, their activities, and their network.

Moreover, international conventions and treaties have been established to address the legal aspects of dirty bomb activities. The United Nations Security Council Resolution 1540, for instance, imposes binding regulations on all nations to prevent non-state actors from acquiring or using nuclear materials for malicious purposes. This resolution has been instrumental in creating legal obligations for states to enhance their domestic legal frameworks against the making of dirty bombs.

Additionally, efforts have been made to develop comprehensive emergency response plans and preparedness strategies. International organizations, such as the World Health Organization (WHO) and the International Civil Aviation Organization (ICAO), have collaborated with national governments to establish guidelines and protocols for responding to dirty bomb incidents. These initiatives aim to minimize the potential damage and ensure effective coordination among different stakeholders in emergency situations.

To deter individuals involved in dirty bomb activities, legal frameworks have been strengthened with stringent penalties. Nations have enacted legislation that imposes severe punishments on those engaged in the procurement, possession, or use of nuclear materials for illicit purposes. These penalties act as a deterrent and send a strong message that such activities will not be tolerated.

Furthermore, research and development efforts have focused on advancing technologies to enhance dirty bomb prevention. Through collaboration among governments, academia, and industry experts, innovative solutions are being explored to improve nuclear materials detection and tracking technologies, cybersecurity measures, radiation detection and monitoring strategies, and security protocols for nuclear facilities and transportation.

In conclusion, international efforts to strengthen legal frameworks are crucial in preventing the making of dirty bombs. Through international cooperation, information sharing, the establishment of treaties and conventions, the development of emergency response plans, and the enactment of stringent penalties, security agents are better equipped to combat this threat. Furthermore, ongoing research and development initiatives contribute to the enhancement of advanced technologies, which further bolster prevention efforts. It is imperative that these international efforts continue to evolve and adapt to the evolving tactics employed by terrorists, ensuring the safety and security of nations worldwide.

Chapter 11: Research and Development of Advanced Technologies to Enhance Dirty Bomb Prevention Efforts

Innovations in Preventing Dirty Bomb Attacks

Introduction:

In recent years, the threat of dirty bomb attacks has been a growing concern for security agents worldwide. The potential for devastating consequences and widespread panic makes it crucial to stay ahead of terrorists seeking to acquire and utilize nuclear materials. This subchapter explores the various innovations and strategies employed by the Department of Homeland Security (DHS) and international partners to prevent dirty bomb attacks.

Nuclear Materials Detection and Tracking Technologies:

The DHS has invested significantly in the development of advanced technologies for nuclear materials detection and tracking. These cutting-edge systems utilize state-of-the-art sensors, artificial intelligence, and machine learning algorithms to identify and locate potential threats. From handheld radiation detectors to sophisticated portal monitors, these innovations enhance security agents' ability to intercept illicit nuclear materials.

Security Protocols for Nuclear Facilities and Transportation:

The DHS has implemented stringent security protocols for nuclear facilities and transportation, ensuring a robust defense against potential attacks. These protocols include the use of advanced access control systems, radiation monitoring devices, and comprehensive background checks for personnel. The integration of biometric technologies and secure communication networks further fortifies these facilities against unauthorized access.

Cybersecurity Measures to Prevent Terrorist Hacking of Nuclear Systems:

Recognizing the evolving threat landscape, the DHS has prioritized cybersecurity measures to prevent terrorist hacking of nuclear systems. This has involved the establishment of dedicated teams to identify vulnerabilities, conduct regular penetration testing, and develop robust encryption protocols. Collaborative efforts with the intelligence community and private sector partners have strengthened cybersecurity defenses and minimized the risk of unauthorized access to critical nuclear infrastructure.

Radiation Detection and Monitoring Strategies:

To effectively counter dirty bomb threats, security agents have adopted innovative radiation detection and monitoring strategies. These include the deployment of mobile radiation detection units, aerial surveillance systems, and the integration of real-time data analysis. By leveraging these strategies, security agents can quickly identify suspicious radiation signatures, track potential threats, and respond swiftly to mitigate the risk of an attack.

Intelligence Gathering on Terrorist Organizations' Interest in Dirty Bombs:

Understanding the intentions and capabilities of terrorist organizations is paramount in preventing dirty bomb attacks. The DHS, along with international partners, has significantly enhanced intelligence gathering efforts to monitor and assess threats. Through improved information sharing and collaboration, security agents can identify emerging trends, track procurement networks, and disrupt potential plots before they materialize.

International Cooperation and Information Sharing on Nuclear Threats:

Recognizing that nuclear threats transcend national borders, the DHS actively engages in international cooperation and information sharing. This comprehensive approach allows for the exchange of intelligence, best practices, and collaborative efforts to prevent dirty bomb attacks. By fostering strong relationships with international partners, security agents can collectively enhance their ability to detect, track, and deter nuclear threats.

Conclusion:

Preventing dirty bomb attacks requires constant innovation and collaboration among security agents and international partners. The DHS's efforts encompass cutting-edge technologies, robust security protocols, cybersecurity measures, intelligence gathering, and public awareness campaigns. By continuously evolving and refining these strategies, security agents can stay one step ahead of terrorists, safeguarding our nations from the devastating consequences of a dirty bomb attack.

Investing in Research and Development for Enhanced Security

In the ever-evolving world of security threats, it is imperative for security agents to stay one step ahead of terrorists and their destructive plans. The making of a dirty bomb is a haunting reality that poses a significant risk to national and global security. To combat this threat, the Department of Homeland Security has recognized the need to invest in research and development (R&D) initiatives to enhance security measures.

One key area of focus is the development of nuclear materials detection and tracking technologies. By investing in cutting-edge technologies, security agents can effectively identify and locate radioactive materials, preventing terrorists from obtaining them for sinister purposes. These advancements enable swift action and apprehension of those involved in illicit activities.

Security protocols for nuclear facilities and transportation are also crucial in mitigating the threat of dirty bombs. R&D efforts should focus on creating robust security systems that protect nuclear facilities from unauthorized access and ensure the safe transportation of nuclear materials. By continuously improving these protocols, security agents can minimize vulnerabilities and enhance overall safety.

In the digital age, cybersecurity measures play a vital role in preventing terrorist hacking of nuclear systems. R&D efforts should concentrate on developing advanced cybersecurity technologies that safeguard critical infrastructure from cyber threats. By fortifying these systems, security agents can prevent unauthorized access and manipulations that could lead to a dirty bomb incident.

Radiation detection and monitoring strategies are essential in detecting the presence of radioactive materials. R&D should aim to enhance the accuracy and efficiency of radiation detection devices, enabling security agents to identify potential threats swiftly. Additionally, developing portable and affordable monitoring tools will empower law enforcement agencies to conduct comprehensive checks in various environments.

Intelligence gathering on terrorist organizations' interest in dirty bombs is essential to preempt potential attacks. By investing in advanced intelligence technologies, security agents can gather critical information on terrorist networks, their intentions, and their capabilities. This knowledge will enable proactive measures and targeted interventions to disrupt their plans.

International cooperation and information sharing on nuclear threats are paramount in combating the global menace of dirty bombs. R&D efforts should focus on developing platforms and protocols that facilitate seamless information exchange between countries. By sharing intelligence, best practices, and technological advancements, security agents can collectively strengthen global security.

Emergency response plans and preparedness for dirty bomb incidents are crucial to minimize the impact of an attack. Investing in R&D initiatives that evaluate and enhance response strategies will equip security agents with the necessary tools to effectively manage and mitigate the consequences of such incidents.

Public awareness campaigns on the dangers of dirty bombs should also be a priority. R&D efforts should aim to develop comprehensive educational materials and initiatives that raise public awareness about the risks and consequences associated with dirty bombs. By educating the public, security agents can foster a sense of vigilance and encourage community involvement in preventing such attacks.

Legal frameworks and penalties for individuals involved in dirty bomb activities also play a critical role in deterring potential perpetrators. R&D efforts should focus on evaluating existing laws and regulations to ensure they are comprehensive and effective. By continuously updating legal frameworks and imposing severe penalties, security agents can create a strong deterrent against involvement in dirty bomb activities.

Finally, investing in R&D for advanced technologies is vital to enhance dirty bomb prevention efforts continually. By exploring emerging technologies, such as artificial intelligence, robotics, and quantum computing, security agents can develop innovative solutions that proactively address evolving threats. These technologies have the potential to revolutionize the field of security and provide unprecedented capabilities in preventing dirty bomb incidents.

In conclusion, investing in research and development is essential for security agents in the fight against dirty bombs. By focusing on various areas such as nuclear materials detection, cybersecurity, intelligence gathering, and public awareness, security agents can enhance their capabilities and stay ahead of terrorists' evolving tactics. Continued investment in R&D will ensure that security measures are proactive, robust, and effective in preventing the making of a dirty bomb.

Future Outlook for Advanced Technologies in Counterterrorism Efforts

The fight against terrorism has always been a top priority for security agents, especially when it comes to the making of a dirty bomb. In recent years, technological advancements have played a crucial role in enhancing counterterrorism efforts. As we look ahead, the future outlook for advanced technologies in this field is promising, offering new tools and strategies to safeguard against the threat of dirty bombs.

One area where advanced technologies are making significant strides is in nuclear materials detection and tracking. With the development of sophisticated sensors and detectors, security agents can now identify and locate nuclear materials more rapidly and accurately. These technologies, along with improved tracking systems, enable authorities to detect any illicit movement of nuclear materials, thereby preventing their misuse.

Moreover, security protocols for nuclear facilities and transportation are continuously evolving. Advanced access control systems, biometric authentication, and surveillance technologies are being implemented to fortify the security of these critical infrastructures. Enhanced screening procedures, including advanced imaging technologies, are also being employed to detect any illicit objects or substances.

As the digital landscape becomes increasingly interconnected, cybersecurity measures are paramount to prevent terrorist hacking of nuclear systems. The future will see the development of robust encryption techniques, advanced intrusion detection systems, and artificial intelligence-based algorithms to identify and neutralize cyber threats effectively.

Radiation detection and monitoring strategies are also being revolutionized by advanced technologies. Miniaturized and portable radiation detectors, coupled with real-time monitoring systems and data analytics, enable security agents to swiftly respond to any radioactive threats and mitigate their impact on public safety.

Intelligence gathering on terrorist organizations' interest in dirty bombs remains a crucial aspect of counterterrorism efforts. Advanced data analysis techniques, including machine learning and predictive analytics, are anticipated to enhance intelligence capabilities, providing security agents with timely insights into potential threats.

Furthermore, international cooperation and information sharing on nuclear threats are vital to combat the global menace of dirty bombs. Advanced communication systems and secure information-sharing platforms will facilitate real-time collaboration between different nations, enabling efficient response and proactive prevention of such incidents.

Emergency response plans and preparedness for dirty bomb incidents will continue to be refined with the integration of advanced technologies. Simulation models and virtual reality training programs will help security agents gain practical experience in handling various scenarios, ensuring a swift and effective response during crisis situations.

To raise public awareness on the dangers of dirty bombs, impactful campaigns utilizing advanced media technologies, such as virtual reality, augmented reality, and social media platforms, will be employed. These campaigns will educate the public about the consequences of dirty bomb incidents and emphasize the importance of collective efforts in preventing such attacks.

Legal frameworks and penalties for individuals involved in dirty bomb activities will also be strengthened. Advanced forensic technologies and evidence collection methodologies will aid in the identification and prosecution of perpetrators, serving as a deterrent for potential offenders.

Finally, research and development of advanced technologies will remain a priority in enhancing dirty bomb prevention efforts. Investments in innovative technologies, such as nanotechnology, robotics, and advanced materials, will lead to the development of novel detection and prevention tools, further strengthening our defenses against this threat.

In conclusion, the future outlook for advanced technologies in counterterrorism efforts is promising. Through the development and implementation of state-of-the-art technologies, security agents will be better equipped to prevent the making of a dirty bomb and protect society from its devastating consequences. The continuous evolution of these technologies, coupled with international cooperation and public awareness, will ensure a safer and more secure future.

Conclusion: Safeguarding Against Dirty Bomb Threats - A Collective Responsibility of Security Agents

In conclusion, the threat of dirty bombs remains a significant concern for security agents worldwide. The making of a dirty bomb poses a grave danger to national security, public safety, and the global community as a whole. However, the Department of Homeland Security and various security agencies have been tirelessly working to prevent the making of dirty bombs by terrorists and protect against potential attacks.

The fight against dirty bomb threats requires a collective responsibility from security agents across various sectors. This subchapter has explored several key areas where security agents play a crucial role in safeguarding against dirty bomb threats.

Nuclear materials detection and tracking technologies are essential in preventing terrorists from acquiring or smuggling radioactive materials. Security agents must stay updated with the latest advancements in this field and collaborate with experts to implement effective detection and tracking systems.

Security protocols for nuclear facilities and transportation are vital to ensuring the safety and security of radioactive materials. Security agents must enforce stringent measures, including access control, surveillance, and regular inspections, to prevent any unauthorized access or potential theft.

Cybersecurity measures play a critical role in preventing terrorists from hacking into nuclear systems and gaining control over radioactive materials. Security agents must work closely with cybersecurity experts to strengthen the resilience of nuclear facilities and prevent any cyber threats.

Radiation detection and monitoring strategies are essential in identifying and containing any potential dirty bomb incidents. Security agents should be adequately trained in radiation detection techniques and equipped with the necessary tools to respond effectively to such situations.

Intelligence gathering on terrorist organizations' interest in dirty bombs is crucial to stay ahead of potential threats. Security agents must collaborate with intelligence agencies and share information to identify and disrupt any plans related to dirty bombs.

International cooperation and information sharing on nuclear threats are vital in preventing the proliferation of dirty bombs. Security agents must actively engage in international forums, share intelligence, and collaborate with other countries to strengthen global security against dirty bomb threats.

Emergency response plans and preparedness for dirty bomb incidents are essential to minimize the impact of an attack. Security agents should participate in regular drills, coordinate with local authorities, and ensure effective communication channels to respond swiftly and efficiently in case of an incident.

Public awareness campaigns on the dangers of dirty bombs are essential to educate and engage the public in the fight against terrorism. Security agents must actively participate in these campaigns, providing accurate information and empowering individuals to report any suspicious activities.

Legal frameworks and penalties for individuals involved in dirty bomb activities play a crucial role in deterring potential perpetrators. Security agents must work closely with legal authorities to ensure strict enforcement of laws and regulations related to dirty bomb activities.

Research and development of advanced technologies are essential in enhancing dirty bomb prevention efforts. Security agents should actively support and participate in research initiatives to develop innovative solutions and technologies to counter the evolving threats.

In conclusion, safeguarding against dirty bomb threats is a collective responsibility of security agents across various domains. By staying informed, collaborating, and actively contributing to prevention efforts, security agents can play a pivotal role in protecting nations and communities from the devastating consequences of dirty bomb attacks. Together, we can build a safer and more secure future.Chapter 1: The Nuclear Club: Current Countries with Nuclear Capabilities

The Early Days of Nuclear Weaponry

Introduction:

The early days of nuclear weaponry marked a defining moment in human history, forever altering the course of warfare, international relations, and global security. This subchapter delves into the fascinating origins of nuclear weapons, exploring the scientific breakthroughs, geopolitical tensions, and technological advancements that paved the way for the creation of these destructive devices.

The Birth of Nuclear Weapons:

The story begins in the early 20th century, with groundbreaking discoveries in nuclear physics by scientists such as Marie Curie, Albert Einstein, and Ernest Rutherford. These pioneers laid the foundation for understanding the immense power that could be harnessed from the atom. However, it was not until the Manhattan Project during World War II that the development of nuclear weapons became a pressing reality.

The Manhattan Project:

Led by the United States, the Manhattan Project brought together the brightest minds in science, engineering, and military strategy to create the world's first atomic bomb. With a sense of urgency driven by the fear of Nazi Germany acquiring such a devastating weapon, research facilities were established, including the famous Los Alamos Laboratory. Under the guidance of physicist J. Robert Oppenheimer, the project successfully produced the first atomic bomb in 1945.

Hiroshima and Nagasaki:

The early days of nuclear weaponry reached a tragic climax when the United States dropped atomic bombs on the Japanese cities of Hiroshima and Nagasaki. The bombings resulted in the deaths of approximately 200,000 people, horrifying the world and forever changing the perception of warfare. The devastation caused by these attacks highlighted the urgent need for international efforts to control and regulate nuclear weapons.

The Nuclear Arms Race:

Following World War II, the United States and the Soviet Union emerged as the dominant superpowers, locked in a tense Cold War. Both nations recognized the strategic advantage that nuclear weapons provided and engaged in a relentless arms race. This arms race led to the development of increasingly advanced and powerful nuclear weapons, including thermonuclear devices capable of mass destruction.

Implications and Consequences:

The early days of nuclear weaponry brought about a paradigm shift in global security and international relations. The emergence of the Nuclear Club, comprising countries possessing nuclear capabilities, created a delicate balance of power known as nuclear deterrence. The threat of mutually assured destruction served as a deterrent against large-scale conflict between nuclear-armed nations. However, it also heightened the risk of accidental nuclear war or nuclear terrorism.

Conclusion:

The early days of nuclear weaponry were marked by scientific breakthroughs, geopolitical tensions, and the tragic use of atomic bombs. The development of these weapons ushered in a new era of global security, characterized by the delicate balance of power and the constant pursuit of nuclear disarmament. Understanding the origins of nuclear weapons is essential for comprehending the challenges and responsibilities faced by the Nuclear Club, as well as the urgent need for non-proliferation efforts and international cooperation in ensuring the safety and security of nuclear technology.

The Pioneers: United States and Soviet Union

The United States and the Soviet Union, two superpowers that emerged from the ashes of World War II, played a pivotal role in shaping the nuclear landscape. This subchapter explores the unique journey of both nations as pioneers in the field of nuclear capabilities.

The United States, with its Manhattan Project, became the first nation to successfully develop and test an atomic bomb. This momentous achievement marked the beginning of the nuclear age. The U.S. utilized its nuclear capabilities to devastating effect during World War II, dropping atomic bombs on the Japanese cities of Hiroshima and Nagasaki. This act forced Japan to surrender and brought an end to the war.

Following the war, the United States continued to invest heavily in nuclear power plants and energy production. Nuclear power emerged as a promising alternative to fossil fuels, offering a clean and efficient source of energy. However, concerns about the safety and environmental impact of nuclear energy led to increased scrutiny and regulations.

The Soviet Union, eager to match the United States' nuclear capabilities, embarked on its own nuclear program. Led by scientists such as Igor Kurchatov, the Soviets successfully tested their first atomic bomb in 1949, signaling their entry into the nuclear club. This development set the stage for the Cold War, a period of intense rivalry and tension between the United States and the Soviet Union.

Nuclear weapons testing and development became a race between the two superpowers, with each seeking to outdo the other in terms of destructive power and technological advancements. This arms race led to the proliferation of nuclear weapons, with other nations like the United Kingdom, France, and China subsequently joining the nuclear club.

While the United States and the Soviet Union engaged in a fierce competition, they also recognized the need for strategic stability and deterrence. This led to the establishment of various treaties and agreements aimed at limiting the spread of nuclear weapons and ensuring nuclear disarmament. The most notable of these is the Treaty on the Non-Proliferation of Nuclear Weapons (NPT), which came into force in 1970.

However, despite efforts towards non-proliferation, incidents and accidents have occurred. The Chernobyl and Fukushima disasters served as wake-up calls, highlighting the potential dangers of nuclear power and the importance of safety measures and emergency preparedness.

Throughout the Cold War, nuclear diplomacy and international relations played a crucial role in preventing a catastrophic conflict. The United States and the Soviet Union engaged in numerous negotiations and summits, such as the Strategic Arms Limitation Talks (SALT), to manage their nuclear arsenals and reduce the risk of accidental nuclear war.

Nuclear espionage and intelligence gathering also played a significant role during this era. Both the United States and the Soviet Union sought to gather information about each other's nuclear capabilities, often resorting to espionage and covert operations.

As we move into the 21st century, the United States and Russia, the successor state to the Soviet Union, continue to possess the largest nuclear arsenals. Modernization efforts and technological advancements have ensured that these weapons remain potent and capable of immense destruction. However, there is also a growing international consensus on the need for nuclear disarmament and the pursuit of a world free from the threat of nuclear weapons.

In conclusion, the United States and the Soviet Union, as pioneers in the field of nuclear capabilities, have left an indelible mark on the nuclear landscape. Their competition, cooperation, and pursuit of strategic stability have shaped the world we live in today. Understanding their history is essential for anyone interested in the nuclear club, energy production, disarmament efforts, international relations, or the impact of nuclear accidents and incidents.

The Expansion: United Kingdom and France

Title: The Expansion: United Kingdom and France

Introduction:

In this subchapter, we will delve into the nuclear capabilities of two prominent nations - the United Kingdom and France. Both countries have played significant roles in shaping the global nuclear landscape. We will explore their nuclear histories, current capabilities, and their influence on international relations. Additionally, we will examine their positions on nuclear disarmament, safety measures, and technological advancements.

1. Nuclear Capabilities and History:

The United Kingdom and France are two of the five recognized nuclear-weapon states under the Treaty on the Non-Proliferation of Nuclear Weapons. The UK became a nuclear power in 1952, while France followed suit in 1960. We will discuss the motivations behind their nuclear programs and the development of their respective arsenals.

2. International Relations and Diplomacy:

The possession of nuclear weapons has given the UK and France significant clout on the world stage. We will explore their roles in international diplomacy, including their participation in nuclear arms control treaties and non-proliferation efforts. Their nuclear capabilities have also influenced their relationships with other nuclear-weapon states and aspiring nations.

3. Nuclear Safety and Emergency Preparedness:

The UK and France have established robust safety measures to ensure the secure operation of their nuclear power plants. We will discuss their emergency preparedness protocols, including the management of potential nuclear accidents or incidents. Lessons learned from past events, such as Chernobyl and Fukushima, have shaped their approach to nuclear safety.

4. Technological Advancements and Modernization:

Both countries have made significant advancements in nuclear technology, including the development of advanced nuclear reactors and submarine-based missile systems. We will explore their efforts in modernizing their nuclear arsenals and the technological advancements they have achieved.

5. Nuclear Disarmament and Non-Proliferation Efforts:

Although possessing nuclear weapons, the UK and France have expressed commitments to disarmament and non-proliferation. We will examine their stances on nuclear disarmament treaties and their efforts to prevent the spread of nuclear weapons technology.

Conclusion:

The nuclear capabilities of the United Kingdom and France have shaped the global nuclear landscape. Their roles in international relations, safety measures, technological advancements, and disarmament efforts have made them key players in promoting stability and security. Understanding their nuclear programs is crucial for comprehending the dynamics of the global nuclear club and the challenges posed by nuclear energy and weapons.

The Unofficial Members: Israel, India, and Pakistan

In the realm of nuclear weapons, there exists a select group known as "The Nuclear Club." This exclusive club consists of countries that possess nuclear capabilities, and their membership is highly coveted and closely monitored by the international community. However, beyond this official club, there are a few unofficial members that have managed to acquire nuclear weapons outside of the established norms. This subchapter focuses on three such unofficial members: Israel, India, and Pakistan.

Israel's nuclear program is shrouded in secrecy, with the country neither confirming nor denying its possession of nuclear weapons. It is widely believed that Israel developed its nuclear arsenal in the 1960s and 1970s, making it the first unofficial member of the Nuclear Club. The Israeli government's policy of ambiguity regarding its nuclear capabilities has led to intense speculation and debate among experts and policymakers.

India, on the other hand, conducted its first nuclear test in 1974, publicly declaring itself a nuclear power. This move surprised the international community and sparked concerns about the balance of power in the region. India's nuclear program has since evolved, and it is currently estimated to possess a significant number of nuclear warheads. Its status as an unofficial member of the Nuclear Club has further complicated the delicate dynamics of South Asian geopolitics.

Pakistan, India's neighbor and historical rival, followed a similar path to acquiring nuclear weapons. In response to India's nuclear tests, Pakistan conducted its own in 1998. This development triggered a new era of arms race and volatility in the region. Pakistan's nuclear program is primarily driven by its desire for deterrence against perceived Indian aggression. However, concerns have been raised about the safety and security of Pakistan's nuclear arsenal, given the country's political instability and the presence of extremist elements.

These unofficial members of the Nuclear Club pose unique challenges to the international community. As non-signatories to the Treaty on the Non-Proliferation of Nuclear Weapons, Israel, India, and Pakistan are not bound by the same obligations and commitments as the official members. This raises questions about global efforts towards nuclear disarmament and non-proliferation.

Furthermore, the presence of these unofficial nuclear powers adds complexities to regional and international relations. Their nuclear capabilities have implications for strategic stability, deterrence, and the likelihood of nuclear conflict. The potential for nuclear accidents, incidents, and espionage also becomes a matter of concern.

In conclusion, while the official Nuclear Club consists of a limited number of countries, there are a few unofficial members that have acquired nuclear weapons. Israel, India, and Pakistan's nuclear programs have significant implications for global security, regional dynamics, and non-proliferation efforts. Understanding the unique challenges posed by these unofficial members is crucial for addressing the various issues related to nuclear power, disarmament, safety, and international relations.

The Newest Entrants: North Korea

North Korea, the secretive and isolated nation, has emerged as one of the most concerning additions to the nuclear club. This subchapter sheds light on North Korea's nuclear capabilities, its impact on global security, and the challenges it poses to international efforts towards disarmament and non-proliferation.

In recent years, North Korea's aggressive pursuit of nuclear weapons has become a significant cause for alarm. Despite international condemnation and economic sanctions, the country has successfully conducted several nuclear tests and developed missile systems capable of reaching distant targets. These advancements have raised concerns about the stability of the region and the potential for a catastrophic conflict.

North Korea's nuclear aspirations have strained diplomatic relations and sparked a series of high-stakes negotiations. The international community has engaged in numerous rounds of talks, aiming to persuade North Korea to abandon its nuclear weapons program. However, progress has been limited, and the regime's insistence on maintaining its nuclear arsenal has remained a major obstacle to achieving a peaceful resolution.

The development of nuclear weapons by North Korea has also heightened concerns about nuclear safety and emergency preparedness. The regime's unpredictable behavior and lack of transparency raise worries about the potential for a nuclear accident or incident. The international community must prioritize efforts to ensure adequate safety measures and emergency response capabilities in the region.

Moreover, North Korea's nuclear advancements have implications for nuclear deterrence and strategic stability. The country's possession of nuclear weapons challenges the existing balance of power in Northeast Asia. It also raises questions about the effectiveness of traditional deterrence strategies and calls for a reassessment of global security frameworks.

As North Korea continues to enhance its nuclear weapons delivery systems, including missiles, submarines, and bombers, its reach and capabilities expand. These developments have significant implications for regional and international security, necessitating closer scrutiny and monitoring of North Korea's activities.

The international community must remain vigilant against nuclear espionage and intelligence gathering by North Korea. The regime's history of illicit activities and clandestine operations underscores the importance of robust intelligence sharing and countermeasures to prevent the proliferation of nuclear technology and materials.

In conclusion, North Korea's entry into the nuclear club poses significant challenges to global security and stability. The regime's pursuit of nuclear weapons undermines international efforts towards disarmament, heightens concerns about nuclear safety, and raises questions about the effectiveness of traditional deterrence strategies. Addressing these challenges requires a coordinated and robust response from the international community to ensure the peaceful resolution of the North Korean nuclear issue.

Chapter 2: The Aspirants and Those Who Publicly Renounced

The Aspiring Nations: Iran and Saudi Arabia

In this subchapter, we will explore two nations that have long been aspiring to join the exclusive club of countries with nuclear capabilities: Iran and Saudi Arabia. These countries have garnered significant attention and concern from the international community due to their potential to disrupt regional and global security dynamics.

Iran, a country with a rich history and a strategic location in the Middle East, has been at the forefront of discussions on nuclear proliferation for decades. The Iranian nuclear program has faced scrutiny and suspicion from the international community, with concerns over its intentions and the possibility of weaponization. Despite Iran's claims of pursuing peaceful nuclear energy, its secretive nature and lack of transparency have fueled doubts and led to sanctions and diplomatic tensions.

Saudi Arabia, on the other hand, is a regional powerhouse that has expressed its aspirations to acquire nuclear capabilities if Iran were to succeed. As the custodian of Islam's holiest sites, Saudi Arabia's pursuit of nuclear weapons could have a significant impact on the regional balance of power. However, the kingdom's motivations and intentions remain unclear, and it has not yet taken concrete steps towards developing its own nuclear program.

The potential nuclear ambitions of both Iran and Saudi Arabia pose numerous challenges and risks. The proliferation of nuclear weapons in the volatile Middle East could trigger a dangerous arms race and heighten tensions among neighboring countries. It could also undermine global efforts for disarmament and non-proliferation, as well as jeopardize the delicate balance of power in the region.

Additionally, the safety and security of nuclear facilities in these aspiring nations are of paramount concern. The Fukushima and Chernobyl disasters serve as stark reminders of the catastrophic consequences that can result from nuclear accidents. As Iran and Saudi Arabia embark on their nuclear journeys, it is crucial that they prioritize safety measures and emergency preparedness to prevent any potential disasters.

Moreover, the international community must engage in robust diplomacy and dialogue to address the nuclear ambitions of Iran and Saudi Arabia. Nuclear deterrence and strategic stability are essential in preventing conflicts and maintaining peace in the region. It is also crucial to monitor and counter potential nuclear espionage and intelligence gathering activities to prevent the misuse of sensitive nuclear technology.

In conclusion, the aspirations of Iran and Saudi Arabia to acquire nuclear capabilities have far-reaching implications for global security. As the international community grapples with the complexities of nuclear power and proliferation, it must strive to find peaceful and diplomatic solutions to address the concerns and aspirations of these two aspiring nations. The future of nuclear diplomacy, non-proliferation efforts, and strategic stability hinges on the effective management of these challenges.

The Former Nuclear Powers: South Africa and Belarus

In the ever-changing landscape of global politics and power dynamics, the issue of nuclear capabilities has always been a sensitive and critical topic. Nuclear weapons, with their immense destructive power, have the ability to shape international relations, deter adversaries, and maintain strategic stability. In this subchapter, we will explore two former nuclear powers – South Africa and Belarus – and delve into the reasons behind their decisions to renounce their nuclear capabilities.

South Africa, once a member of the exclusive nuclear club, made headlines in the 1990s when it voluntarily dismantled its nuclear weapons program. This move came as a surprise to the international community, as South Africa had managed to develop a small arsenal of nuclear warheads in secret. The decision to renounce nuclear weapons was largely driven by the country's transition to democracy and the dismantling of its apartheid regime. South Africa's leaders recognized that nuclear disarmament would not only promote peace and stability in the region but also enhance its image on the global stage.

Belarus, on the other hand, inherited nuclear weapons from the Soviet Union after its dissolution in 1991. However, the newly independent nation faced numerous challenges in maintaining its nuclear arsenal. The cost of operating and securing these weapons became a burden for Belarus, and the government realized that it would be more prudent to renounce its nuclear capabilities. With the signing of the Treaty on the Non-Proliferation of Nuclear Weapons, Belarus committed itself to disarmament and non-proliferation efforts, setting an example for other countries in similar situations.

The decisions of South Africa and Belarus to renounce their nuclear capabilities highlight the importance of nuclear disarmament and non-proliferation efforts. These countries recognized that possessing nuclear weapons did not guarantee security and stability. Instead, they opted for a diplomatic approach, focusing on building strong international relations and fostering trust among nations. By abandoning their nuclear weapons programs, South Africa and Belarus contributed to the global efforts aimed at reducing the number of nuclear-armed states and preventing the spread of nuclear weapons technology.

The cases of South Africa and Belarus also shed light on the challenges associated with nuclear weapons modernization and technological advancements. Both countries faced difficulties in maintaining and upgrading their nuclear arsenals, realizing that the costs and risks outweighed the benefits. Their experiences serve as a reminder that nuclear weapons are not only a potential threat to international security but also a significant financial burden.

In conclusion, the decisions made by South Africa and Belarus to renounce their nuclear capabilities provide valuable insights into the complex dynamics of nuclear disarmament and non-proliferation. These former nuclear powers serve as role models for countries aspiring to join the nuclear club, demonstrating that diplomatic efforts and trust-building can pave the way towards a more secure and peaceful world. By understanding the challenges and consequences associated with nuclear weapons, we can continue to work towards a future free from the threat of nuclear warfare.

The Renouncers: Ukraine and Kazakhstan

In the complex world of nuclear capabilities, two countries stand out for their decision to renounce nuclear weapons: Ukraine and Kazakhstan. This subchapter explores the reasons behind their choices and the implications of their renunciation.

Ukraine, once part of the Soviet Union, inherited a significant nuclear arsenal after the dissolution of the USSR. However, in a historic move, Ukraine decided to give up its nuclear weapons in 1994. This decision was motivated by several factors, including the desire to improve relations with the international community and to ensure its own security in a post-Cold War era.

By renouncing nuclear weapons, Ukraine gained international recognition as a responsible and non-proliferating state. This move also paved the way for improved diplomatic relations with neighboring countries and the European Union. Furthermore, it allowed Ukraine to focus on its economic development and to redirect its resources towards other pressing issues.

Kazakhstan, another former Soviet republic, also made the bold decision to renounce nuclear weapons. Kazakhstan inherited the fourth-largest nuclear arsenal in the world after the collapse of the USSR. However, it voluntarily gave up its nuclear weapons and joined the Treaty on the Non-Proliferation of Nuclear Weapons as a non-nuclear weapon state.

Kazakhstan's decision to renounce nuclear weapons was driven by a commitment to global nuclear disarmament and non-proliferation efforts. By doing so, Kazakhstan became a role model for other countries and contributed significantly to regional stability. Moreover, this decision showcased Kazakhstan's commitment to its citizens' safety and to the peaceful use of nuclear energy.

Both Ukraine and Kazakhstan have faced numerous challenges since renouncing nuclear weapons. They have had to rely on international assistance to ensure the safe dismantlement and disposal of their nuclear arsenals. Additionally, these countries have actively participated in nuclear disarmament negotiations and have advocated for non-proliferation efforts.

The cases of Ukraine and Kazakhstan demonstrate that renouncing nuclear weapons can bring about significant benefits, including improved international relations and enhanced security. These countries serve as examples for other nations considering renunciation, and their experiences highlight the importance of diplomatic efforts, international cooperation, and the pursuit of peaceful nuclear energy production.

As the world continues to grapple with nuclear safety, disarmament, and non-proliferation, the stories of Ukraine and Kazakhstan provide valuable insights into the challenges and rewards of renouncing nuclear weapons. Their experiences serve as a reminder of the importance of international collaboration and the pursuit of a safer and more secure world.

Chapter 3: Nuclear Power Plants and Energy Production

Nuclear Power Plants: A Brief Overview

Nuclear power plants have become a significant source of energy production in many countries around the world. This subchapter aims to provide a comprehensive understanding of nuclear power plants, their benefits, associated risks, and global efforts to ensure their safe and responsible operation.

Nuclear power plants harness the energy released from nuclear reactions to generate electricity. They work by utilizing a controlled chain reaction of nuclear fission, where the nucleus of an atom is split into two smaller nuclei, releasing an enormous amount of energy. This energy is then converted into electricity that can power homes, industries, and communities.

One of the major advantages of nuclear power plants is their ability to produce large amounts of electricity without emitting greenhouse gases or contributing to air pollution. This makes them a promising alternative to fossil fuels, which are major contributors to global warming and climate change. Moreover, nuclear power is a reliable and consistent source of energy, ensuring a stable power supply even during peak demand periods.

However, nuclear power plants also pose significant risks if not operated with utmost care and adherence to safety protocols. The potential for accidents, such as the infamous Chernobyl and Fukushima incidents, highlights the importance of stringent safety measures and emergency preparedness in the nuclear industry. The subchapter will delve into these accidents, analyzing their causes, consequences, and the lessons learned to prevent future mishaps.

In addition to safety concerns, the development and testing of nuclear weapons remain a grave global issue. The subchapter will explore the connection between nuclear power plants and nuclear weapons programs, as well as the ongoing efforts towards nuclear disarmament, non-proliferation, and arms control. It will discuss the role of international organizations like the International Atomic Energy Agency (IAEA) in monitoring and regulating the peaceful use of nuclear energy.

Furthermore, the subchapter will touch upon the diplomatic and strategic aspects of nuclear power plants, including nuclear deterrence, international relations, and the modernization of nuclear weapons and delivery systems. It will also shed light on the controversial subjects of nuclear espionage and intelligence gathering, emphasizing the need for transparency and trust among nations.

Overall, this subchapter aims to provide the public with a comprehensive overview of nuclear power plants, their benefits, associated risks, and global efforts to ensure their safe and responsible operation. It will serve as a valuable resource for those interested in understanding the complexities and challenges of the nuclear industry, as well as the broader implications of nuclear power in a rapidly changing world.

Leading Nuclear Energy Producers: United States and France

The United States and France are two of the leading nations in the field of nuclear energy production. Both countries have invested heavily in the development of nuclear power plants and have made significant contributions to the advancement of nuclear technology.

In the United States, nuclear energy plays a crucial role in the country's overall energy mix. The U.S. currently operates the largest number of nuclear power plants in the world, with a total of 93 reactors spread across 28 states. These reactors generate approximately 20% of the country's total electricity, making nuclear energy the second-largest source of power after natural gas.

The U.S. nuclear industry has a long history of innovation and technological advancements. It was the United States that first demonstrated the potential of nuclear energy with the successful development and deployment of the world's first nuclear power plant in Shippingport, Pennsylvania, in 1957. Since then, the U.S. has continued to invest in research and development, leading to improved reactor designs, enhanced safety measures, and greater efficiency in electricity generation.

France, on the other hand, is renowned for its strong commitment to nuclear power. The country heavily relies on nuclear energy for its electricity needs, with approximately 70% of its total power coming from nuclear reactors. France operates 56 nuclear reactors, making it the second-largest producer of nuclear energy in the world.

The French nuclear industry is known for its advanced reactor technology and expertise in the entire nuclear fuel cycle. The country has developed its own unique reactor design, known as the pressurized water reactor (PWR), which has gained international recognition for its safety features and operational efficiency. France also has a robust infrastructure for the reprocessing of nuclear fuel, allowing for the recycling and reuse of spent fuel, which contributes to the sustainability of its nuclear program.

Both the United States and France have made significant contributions to nuclear safety and emergency preparedness. They have implemented rigorous safety regulations and protocols to ensure the safe operation of nuclear power plants and to mitigate the risks associated with nuclear energy production. Additionally, both countries actively participate in international efforts for nuclear disarmament and non-proliferation, advocating for the reduction of nuclear weapons stockpiles and promoting peaceful uses of nuclear energy.

As leading nuclear energy producers, the United States and France have played pivotal roles in shaping the global nuclear landscape. Their advancements in technology, commitment to safety, and active participation in international discussions have contributed to the overall progress of nuclear energy production and the promotion of peace and security in the nuclear domain.

Growing Nuclear Energy Demand: China and India

China and India, two of the world's most populous countries, are experiencing a significant increase in their demand for nuclear energy. As they strive to meet their respective energy needs, both nations are turning to nuclear power as a viable and sustainable solution. This subchapter will delve into the reasons behind the growing nuclear energy demand in China and India and its implications for the global nuclear landscape.

China, with its rapidly expanding economy, has been actively investing in nuclear power plants to meet its burgeoning energy requirements. The country's nuclear energy sector has witnessed remarkable growth over the past decade, with plans to triple its nuclear capacity by 2030. China's commitment to nuclear energy is driven by several factors, including reducing its reliance on fossil fuels, mitigating air pollution, and meeting its ambitious carbon reduction targets. Furthermore, nuclear power provides a stable and reliable source of energy that can support the country's industrial growth and urbanization.

Similarly, India, with its ever-increasing population and economic development, is also turning to nuclear energy to address its energy demands. The Indian government has set an ambitious target of achieving 40% of its electricity generation from non-fossil fuel sources by 2030, and nuclear power plays a crucial role in achieving this goal. India's nuclear energy program aims to enhance energy security, reduce greenhouse gas emissions, and provide electricity to millions of people who currently lack access to reliable power.

The growing nuclear energy demand in China and India has significant implications for the global nuclear landscape. As both countries expand their nuclear capabilities, they become key players in the international nuclear market. This development presents opportunities for collaboration with other nuclear-capable nations and for the transfer of nuclear technology and expertise. However, it also raises concerns regarding nuclear safety, emergency preparedness, and non-proliferation efforts. The international community must closely monitor the nuclear activities of China and India to ensure that they comply with global nuclear standards and regulations.

In conclusion, the growing nuclear energy demand in China and India reflects their commitment to meeting their energy needs in a sustainable and environmentally friendly manner. While this presents opportunities for economic development and energy security, it also poses challenges in terms of nuclear safety, non-proliferation, and international cooperation. The global community must engage with China and India to ensure the responsible and safe growth of their nuclear energy programs while addressing concerns related to proliferation and safety.

Nuclear Energy and Sustainability

In recent years, the topic of nuclear energy and sustainability has gained significant attention worldwide. As we navigate an era of increasing environmental concerns and the need for clean and renewable energy sources, it is crucial to understand the role of nuclear power in achieving a sustainable future. This subchapter aims to provide an overview of nuclear energy's impact on sustainability and its relevance to various stakeholders, including current nuclear countries, aspirants, and those who publicly renounced nuclear capabilities.

Nuclear power plants and energy production have emerged as a viable alternative to fossil fuel-based energy generation. Unlike coal or natural gas-fired power plants, nuclear reactors produce electricity without emitting greenhouse gases, contributing to the reduction of carbon emissions. With the potential to generate large amounts of electricity consistently, nuclear power can address the growing global demand for energy while minimizing the environmental impact.

However, nuclear energy's sustainability is not without its challenges. Nuclear disarmament and non-proliferation efforts are vital to prevent the misuse of nuclear technology for destructive purposes. The subchapter will explore the delicate balance between harnessing nuclear energy for peaceful purposes and ensuring that it does not fall into the wrong hands.

Furthermore, nuclear safety and emergency preparedness remain critical aspects of sustainable nuclear energy. Drawing lessons from past incidents such as Chernobyl and Fukushima, the subchapter will delve into the measures taken to enhance safety standards, improve reactor designs, and establish effective emergency response systems.

The exploration of nuclear diplomacy and international relations is also pertinent in understanding the sustainable use of nuclear energy. The nuclear club, comprising countries with nuclear capabilities, plays a crucial role in shaping global nuclear policies, cooperation, and non-proliferation efforts. The subchapter will shed light on the dynamics of nuclear diplomacy and its impact on sustainable nuclear energy practices.

Nuclear deterrence and strategic stability will also be discussed in relation to nuclear energy and sustainability. The subchapter will explore the role of nuclear weapons delivery systems, such as missiles, submarines, and bombers, in maintaining stability among nuclear-armed nations and safeguarding against potential threats.

Additionally, the subchapter will touch upon nuclear weapons modernization and technological advancements, as well as the challenges posed by nuclear espionage and intelligence gathering. These areas have a direct impact on the sustainability of nuclear energy and the overall security landscape.

Finally, the subchapter will address nuclear accidents and incidents, including in-depth analysis of major disasters like Chernobyl and Fukushima. Understanding the causes, consequences, and lessons learned from such incidents is crucial to ensuring that nuclear energy remains a sustainable and safe option.

In conclusion, this subchapter on nuclear energy and sustainability aims to provide an extensive overview of the various dimensions surrounding nuclear power. It seeks to inform and engage the public, as well as those directly involved in the nuclear club, by addressing key topics such as energy production, disarmament, safety, diplomacy, and environmental impact. By exploring these areas, we can foster a better understanding of how nuclear energy can contribute to a sustainable future while addressing the concerns and challenges associated with its use.

Chapter 4: Nuclear Disarmament and Non-Proliferation Efforts

The Treaty on the Non-Proliferation of Nuclear Weapons (NPT)

The Treaty on the Non-Proliferation of Nuclear Weapons (NPT) is an international treaty aimed at preventing the spread of nuclear weapons and promoting disarmament. It was opened for signature in 1968 and entered into force in 1970. The NPT is considered one of the cornerstones of nuclear disarmament and non-proliferation efforts.

The NPT has three main pillars: non-proliferation, disarmament, and the peaceful use of nuclear energy. Under the treaty, non-nuclear-weapon states commit to not acquiring nuclear weapons, while nuclear-weapon states commit to disarmament and to provide assistance in developing peaceful nuclear energy programs.

The NPT has been successful in preventing the further spread of nuclear weapons. Currently, there are only nine countries known to possess nuclear weapons: the United States, Russia, the United Kingdom, France, China, India, Pakistan, Israel, and North Korea. These countries are often referred to as the "nuclear club." The NPT has also encouraged countries to renounce their nuclear weapons aspirations, such as South Africa, Ukraine, and Kazakhstan.

The treaty has played a crucial role in promoting nuclear safety and emergency preparedness. It has established guidelines and standards for the safe operation of nuclear power plants and the handling of nuclear materials. The NPT also encourages countries to share information and cooperate in the event of nuclear accidents or incidents, as seen in the aftermath of the Chernobyl and Fukushima disasters.

In the realm of international relations, the NPT has fostered nuclear diplomacy and helped maintain strategic stability. The treaty promotes dialogue and negotiations among nuclear-weapon states and non-nuclear-weapon states, reducing the likelihood of nuclear conflict. It has also led to the development of arms control agreements and treaties, such as the Strategic Arms Reduction Treaty (START) between the United States and Russia.

The NPT has faced challenges, including concerns about nuclear weapons modernization and technological advancements. Some argue that nuclear-weapon states are not doing enough to fulfill their disarmament obligations under the treaty. Additionally, there have been instances of nuclear espionage and intelligence gathering, highlighting the need for robust safeguards and monitoring mechanisms.

Overall, the NPT remains a crucial instrument in preventing the proliferation of nuclear weapons and promoting disarmament. It continues to shape international efforts towards nuclear non-proliferation, nuclear safety, and peaceful nuclear energy. As the world grapples with the complex issues surrounding nuclear weapons, the NPT provides a framework for dialogue, cooperation, and the pursuit of a safer and more secure world.

Nuclear Disarmament Initiatives and Treaties

In a world where the threat of nuclear weapons looms large, the importance of nuclear disarmament initiatives and treaties cannot be overstated. These international agreements represent the collective effort of nations to reduce and eliminate nuclear weapons, promoting peace and global security. This subchapter delves into the various initiatives and treaties that have shaped the nuclear disarmament landscape.

The Non-Proliferation Treaty (NPT) stands as the bedrock of disarmament efforts. It aims to prevent the spread of nuclear weapons, promote disarmament, and foster the peaceful use of nuclear energy. As of now, 191 countries have become party to the NPT, demonstrating a global consensus on the importance of curbing nuclear proliferation.

Another milestone in disarmament efforts is the Treaty on the Prohibition of Nuclear Weapons (TPNW). This treaty, adopted in 2017, seeks to comprehensively prohibit the development, testing, production, acquisition, possession, and use of nuclear weapons. While not yet universally embraced, the TPNW represents a significant step towards a nuclear-free world.

Additionally, bilateral disarmament agreements have played a crucial role. The Strategic Arms Reduction Treaty (START) between the United States and Russia, for instance, has led to substantial reductions in deployed strategic nuclear weapons. Such agreements demonstrate the commitment of these nuclear superpowers to reducing the risk of nuclear conflict.

Furthermore, nuclear-weapon-free zones (NWFZ) have emerged as regional efforts to advance disarmament. These zones, such as the Treaty of Tlatelolco in Latin America and the Caribbean, prohibit the production, acquisition, or deployment of nuclear weapons within their respective territories. NWFZs foster regional stability and contribute to global disarmament efforts.

However, challenges persist. Some nations argue that nuclear weapons serve as a deterrent, ensuring their security in an increasingly complex geopolitical landscape. Others highlight the risks associated with disarmament, fearing potential vulnerabilities if they relinquish their nuclear capabilities.

Nevertheless, the urgency of disarmament and non-proliferation efforts cannot be ignored. The catastrophic consequences of a nuclear conflict serve as a stark reminder of the need for progress in this arena. By strengthening existing initiatives, fostering dialogue, and encouraging greater participation, the international community can work towards a world free of nuclear weapons.

As members of the public, it is crucial to educate ourselves about nuclear disarmament initiatives and treaties. By understanding the complexities and implications of these efforts, we can contribute to informed discussions and advocate for a safer world. Together, we can support the aspirations of countries seeking to renounce nuclear capabilities, champion nuclear safety and emergency preparedness, and promote peace through disarmament.

Challenges and Controversies in Non-Proliferation Efforts

In the realm of international relations, few issues capture the attention and concern of the public as much as nuclear weapons and their proliferation. As the world grapples with the ever-present threat of nuclear conflict, the challenges and controversies surrounding non-proliferation efforts have become increasingly significant. This subchapter explores the complex dynamics and contentious issues that arise in the pursuit of preventing the spread of nuclear weapons.

One of the primary challenges in non-proliferation efforts is the existence of countries with nuclear capabilities. The Nuclear Club, comprising the United States, Russia, China, France, and the United Kingdom, possesses immense military power, but their status as nuclear states raises questions about equity and disarmament. Critics argue that these nations have failed to fulfill their obligations under the Treaty on the Non-Proliferation of Nuclear Weapons (NPT), while proponents argue that their nuclear arsenals serve as a deterrent against potential aggressors.

Another controversy surrounds the aspirations of countries seeking to acquire nuclear weapons. The public and international community closely monitor the actions of states like North Korea and Iran, whose nuclear ambitions have provoked global concern. The delicate balance between diplomatic negotiations, economic sanctions, and military posturing highlights the difficulties in preventing the spread of nuclear weapons in an increasingly volatile world.

Furthermore, the issue of nuclear safety and emergency preparedness has gained prominence in recent years. The devastating accidents at Chernobyl and Fukushima serve as stark reminders of the catastrophic consequences of mishandling nuclear technology. The public demands greater transparency and robust safety protocols to ensure that nuclear power plants and facilities are effectively managed and that emergency response systems are in place.

Nuclear espionage and intelligence gathering present additional challenges to non-proliferation efforts. The public is often unaware of the covert operations and intelligence activities that take place in the pursuit of nuclear weapons-related information. The delicate balance between national security and international cooperation in intelligence sharing raises ethical and legal dilemmas.

In conclusion, the challenges and controversies surrounding non-proliferation efforts are manifold and require the attention and engagement of the public. By understanding the complexities of nuclear power, disarmament, safety, and international relations, individuals can actively participate in the ongoing debate and contribute to the pursuit of a safer and more secure world. It is through informed discussions and collective action that the international community can effectively address the challenges posed by nuclear weapons and work towards a future free from the threat of nuclear conflict.

Chapter 5: Nuclear Weapons Testing and Development

The Era of Nuclear Testing

In the mid-20th century, the world witnessed the dawn of a new era in history: the era of nuclear testing. This subchapter explores the significance of nuclear testing, its impact on international relations, and its implications for global security.

Nuclear testing refers to the detonation of nuclear devices, either underground, in the atmosphere, or underwater, to evaluate their effectiveness and destructive power. It started with the United States' Trinity test in July 1945, followed by the bombings of Hiroshima and Nagasaki. This event marked the beginning of the nuclear age and forever changed the course of history.

During the Cold War, nuclear testing became a symbol of power and deterrence. The race for nuclear weapons between the United States and the Soviet Union led to an intensive testing period. The two superpowers conducted hundreds of tests, both in the atmosphere and underground, showcasing their military capabilities to the world.

The era of nuclear testing was not limited to the superpowers. Other countries, such as the United Kingdom, France, and China, joined the nuclear club and conducted their own tests. These tests were often met with global concern and condemnation due to the radioactive fallout and environmental impacts they caused.

The implications of nuclear testing extended beyond military capabilities. It also had significant effects on international diplomacy and non-proliferation efforts. The Comprehensive Nuclear-Test-Ban

Treaty (CTBT) was adopted in 1996 to ban all nuclear explosions, but it has yet to be fully ratified by all nuclear-capable countries.

Furthermore, the era of nuclear testing highlighted the need for nuclear safety and emergency preparedness. Accidents like the Chernobyl and Fukushima disasters demonstrated the devastating consequences of nuclear energy gone wrong. These incidents exacerbated global concerns about the safety of nuclear power plants and the potential for nuclear accidents.

Nuclear espionage and intelligence gathering also played a significant role during this era. Countries engaged in espionage activities to gather information about each other's nuclear capabilities, which further escalated tensions and mistrust between nations.

As the era of nuclear testing came to an end, efforts towards nuclear disarmament and non-proliferation gained momentum. International agreements and treaties aimed to reduce the number of nuclear weapons and prevent their spread to other countries.

In conclusion, the era of nuclear testing was a defining period in human history. It showcased the destructive power of nuclear weapons, shaped international relations, and raised concerns about nuclear safety and proliferation. Understanding this era is crucial for anyone interested in the nuclear club, nuclear disarmament, energy production, and the geopolitical landscape of the modern world.

Current Nuclear Weapons Development Programs

In this subchapter, we will explore the various nuclear weapons development programs that are currently underway in different countries around the world. It is important for the public to have an understanding of these programs as they directly impact global security and stability.

One of the most well-known nuclear weapons development programs is that of North Korea. Despite international condemnation and sanctions, North Korea has been actively pursuing the development of nuclear weapons. They conducted their first nuclear test in 2006 and have since carried out several more, demonstrating their commitment to advancing their nuclear capabilities.

Another country with an active nuclear weapons program is Iran. Although Iran claims that their nuclear program is for peaceful purposes, such as energy production, there are concerns that they are seeking to develop nuclear weapons. This has led to international efforts to monitor and limit Iran's nuclear activities through agreements like the Joint Comprehensive Plan of Action (JCPOA).

While some countries are actively developing nuclear weapons, others have renounced their nuclear capabilities. For example, South Africa voluntarily dismantled its nuclear weapons program in the early 1990s, becoming the first country to do so. This decision was seen as a positive step towards global disarmament and non-proliferation efforts.

In addition to the current countries with nuclear capabilities, there are also countries aspiring to develop nuclear weapons. One such country is Saudi Arabia, which has expressed interest in acquiring nuclear technology for peaceful purposes. However, there are concerns that this could potentially lead to a nuclear arms race in the Middle East.

It is essential to closely monitor nuclear weapons development programs to ensure that they do not pose a threat to global security. International efforts, such as the Treaty on the Non-Proliferation of Nuclear Weapons (NPT), aim to prevent the proliferation of nuclear weapons and promote disarmament.

In conclusion, understanding the current nuclear weapons development programs is crucial for the public in order to comprehend the complex and interconnected issues surrounding nuclear power plants and energy production, nuclear disarmament and non-proliferation efforts, nuclear weapons testing and development, nuclear safety and emergency preparedness, nuclear diplomacy and international relations, nuclear deterrence and strategic stability, nuclear weapons delivery systems, nuclear weapons modernization and technological advancements, nuclear espionage and intelligence gathering, and nuclear accidents and incidents. By staying informed, individuals can actively contribute to discussions and actions aimed at promoting a safer and more secure world.

Nuclear Weapons and Technological Advancements

In the modern world, technological advancements have played a significant role in shaping the capabilities and threats associated with nuclear weapons. As we delve into the subchapter titled "Nuclear Weapons and Technological Advancements," we aim to shed light on the intersection between nuclear weapons and the rapid progress of technology. This chapter will be of particular interest to the public, including those with a curiosity about the nuclear club, current nuclear countries, aspirants, and those who have publicly renounced nuclear weapons. It will also appeal to individuals interested in nuclear power plants and energy production, nuclear disarmament and non-proliferation efforts, nuclear weapons testing and development, nuclear safety and emergency preparedness, nuclear diplomacy and international relations, nuclear deterrence and strategic stability, nuclear weapons delivery systems, nuclear weapons modernization and technological advancements, nuclear espionage and intelligence gathering, as well as nuclear accidents and incidents.

Technological advancements have significantly influenced the development and modernization of nuclear weapons. From the early days of the Manhattan Project to the present, scientists and engineers have harnessed cutting-edge technology to enhance the destructive power, accuracy, and efficiency of nuclear weapons. The evolution of delivery systems, including missiles, submarines, and bombers, has allowed for more effective deployment and increased the range of nuclear capabilities possessed by various countries.

Moreover, technological advancements have also played a crucial role in ensuring nuclear safety and emergency preparedness. Lessons learned from tragic incidents like Chernobyl and Fukushima have led to improved safety protocols, enhanced reactor designs, and more efficient emergency response mechanisms. The public, as well as policymakers, must be aware of these advancements to better understand the measures taken to prevent and mitigate nuclear accidents.

Furthermore, nuclear espionage and intelligence gathering have become increasingly sophisticated due to technological advancements. The development of surveillance technologies, including satellites and advanced monitoring systems, has allowed countries to monitor the activities of potential nuclear proliferators and ensure treaty compliance. Additionally, advancements in cyber warfare have introduced a new dimension to nuclear espionage, with the potential to disrupt critical infrastructure and compromise the security of nuclear systems.

As we explore the relationship between nuclear weapons and technological advancements, it becomes evident that while technology has facilitated progress in various aspects of nuclear capabilities, it has also presented new challenges and risks. It is essential for the public and policymakers to stay informed about these advancements to ensure responsible decision-making, promote nuclear disarmament and non-proliferation efforts, and advocate for the safe and secure use of nuclear energy.

In conclusion, the subchapter "Nuclear Weapons and Technological Advancements" provides a comprehensive overview of the intersection between nuclear weapons and technological progress. It addresses the interests of the public and various niches, including the nuclear club, current nuclear countries, aspirants, and those who have renounced nuclear weapons. By understanding the role of technology in nuclear power, safety, diplomacy, and intelligence, we can better navigate the complexities of nuclear weapons in the modern world.

Chapter 6: Nuclear Safety and Emergency Preparedness

Safety Measures in Nuclear Power Plants

Nuclear power plants play a crucial role in meeting the world's energy demands. However, they also pose potential risks if not operated and maintained with utmost safety. This subchapter aims to shed light on the safety measures implemented in nuclear power plants to ensure the protection of the public, workers, and the environment.

Firstly, one of the primary safety measures is the use of multiple barriers to prevent the release of radioactive materials. Nuclear reactors are designed with multiple layers of protection, including fuel cladding, reactor coolant systems, and containment buildings. These barriers are constantly monitored and inspected to ensure their integrity.

Additionally, strict regulations and industry standards govern the operation of nuclear power plants. Regulatory bodies are responsible for ensuring that plant operators comply with safety guidelines and maintain the highest safety standards. Regular inspections and audits are conducted to identify any potential issues and address them promptly.

Furthermore, comprehensive emergency preparedness plans are in place to handle any unforeseen incidents. These plans include procedures for evacuating nearby areas, notification systems to alert the public, and coordination with local authorities and emergency response teams. Regular drills and exercises are conducted to test the effectiveness of these plans and identify areas for improvement.

Moreover, continuous training and education are provided to all personnel working in nuclear power plants. This includes both theoretical and practical training on safety procedures, radiation protection, and emergency response. By ensuring that all staff are well-trained and knowledgeable, the risks associated with human error are minimized.

Another crucial safety measure is the sharing of information and lessons learned from past incidents. The nuclear industry has established platforms for the exchange of knowledge and best practices among operators, regulators, and international organizations. This collective learning helps in identifying potential vulnerabilities and implementing preventive measures.

Lastly, advancements in technology have significantly contributed to enhancing safety in nuclear power plants. The development of advanced monitoring systems, computer simulations, and robotics have improved the ability to detect and mitigate potential risks. Additionally, research and development efforts are focused on developing more efficient and safer reactor designs.

In conclusion, nuclear power plants prioritize safety through the implementation of multiple barriers, adherence to strict regulations, emergency preparedness plans, continuous training, knowledge sharing, and technological advancements. These safety measures are essential to ensure the protection of the public, workers, and the environment, and to maintain the viability of nuclear energy as a sustainable and clean energy source.

Handling Nuclear Waste: Storage and Disposal

Nuclear power plants play a significant role in the production of electricity worldwide. However, along with the benefits of nuclear energy comes the challenge of handling and disposing of nuclear waste. This subchapter aims to shed light on the critical aspects of storage and disposal of nuclear waste, providing information for the general public and specific niches such as current nuclear countries, aspirants, and those who renounced nuclear capabilities.

Nuclear waste refers to the radioactive materials that are produced during nuclear reactions in power plants. This waste can remain hazardous for thousands of years, necessitating careful management to protect human health and the environment. The storage and disposal of nuclear waste are crucial to prevent potential accidents, contamination, and unauthorized access to these materials.

Storage of nuclear waste typically involves two approaches: interim storage and permanent disposal. Interim storage facilities, usually located at or near nuclear power plants, provide temporary containment for spent fuel assemblies. These facilities utilize robust containment structures and cooling systems to ensure the safe storage of radioactive waste. However, it is important to note that interim storage is not a long-term solution and should be followed by permanent disposal.

Permanent disposal of nuclear waste is a complex and highly regulated process. Deep geological repositories are considered the most suitable option for long-term disposal. These repositories are constructed deep underground in stable rock formations, providing a natural barrier against the release of radioactive materials. Extensive research and stringent safety assessments are conducted before selecting a site for a repository.

International efforts are ongoing to develop standardized protocols and guidelines for the storage and disposal of nuclear waste. Organizations such as the International Atomic Energy Agency (IAEA) and the World Nuclear Association (WNA) collaborate with member states to ensure the safe management of nuclear waste. These efforts include sharing best practices, conducting research, and promoting international cooperation.

Public awareness and engagement are vital in addressing concerns and misconceptions surrounding nuclear waste. Governments, nuclear industry stakeholders, and non-governmental organizations should actively involve the public in decision-making processes regarding storage and disposal methods. Transparency and open communication are key to building trust and fostering a better understanding of the risks and benefits associated with nuclear waste management.

In conclusion, the proper handling of nuclear waste is of paramount importance to ensure the safety and security of present and future generations. Storage and disposal methods must meet strict safety standards to prevent accidents, contamination, and unauthorized access. International collaboration and public engagement are essential in developing effective strategies for the storage and disposal of nuclear waste. By addressing these challenges, we can maximize the benefits of nuclear energy while minimizing its potential risks.

Emergency Preparedness and Response

In a world where nuclear capabilities are a reality, it is crucial for the public to be informed and prepared for any potential emergencies that may arise. This subchapter will focus on emergency preparedness and response in the context of nuclear incidents, providing essential information to the general public.

Nuclear power plants and energy production pose inherent risks, and it is important to understand the safety measures in place. The subchapter will delve into the protocols followed by countries with nuclear capabilities to prevent accidents and ensure the safe operation of power plants. It will also discuss the potential consequences of a nuclear accident and how emergency response teams are trained and equipped to handle such situations.

Furthermore, the subchapter will explore international efforts towards nuclear disarmament and non-proliferation. It will highlight the importance of diplomatic negotiations and agreements aimed at reducing the number of nuclear weapons globally. The audience will gain insights into the challenges associated with achieving disarmament and the role of international organizations in facilitating discussions.

The subchapter will also shed light on nuclear weapons testing and development, emphasizing the risks and implications of such activities. It will examine the effects of nuclear weapons on the environment and human health, emphasizing the need for responsible testing practices.

In the event of a nuclear emergency, the public must be aware of the appropriate response measures. The subchapter will provide guidance on evacuation procedures, sheltering, and accessing reliable sources of information. It will emphasize the importance of preparedness, including the creation of emergency kits and communication plans.

Additionally, the subchapter will touch on the topic of nuclear espionage and intelligence gathering. It will explore the history of covert operations related to nuclear capabilities and highlight the measures taken to counter such activities.

Finally, the subchapter will examine past nuclear accidents and incidents, such as Chernobyl and Fukushima, and the lessons learned from these disasters. It will emphasize the importance of implementing enhanced safety measures and investing in technological advancements to prevent future incidents.

Overall, this subchapter on emergency preparedness and response aims to provide the public with comprehensive information on nuclear incidents and the measures in place to mitigate risks. By understanding the challenges and precautions associated with nuclear capabilities, the audience will be better equipped to make informed decisions and ensure their safety in an ever-evolving world.

Chapter 7: Nuclear Diplomacy and International Relations

Nuclear Diplomacy: A Historical Perspective

In the realm of international relations, nuclear diplomacy has played a significant role in shaping the world order. This subchapter aims to provide a historical perspective on nuclear diplomacy, tracing its origins and evolution, and examining its impact on international relations.

From the inception of the atomic age with the bombings of Hiroshima and Nagasaki in 1945, nuclear weapons became a central feature of global politics. The subsequent Cold War between the United States and the Soviet Union intensified the need for diplomacy and strategic negotiations. The development of nuclear weapons by these two superpowers ushered in an era of deterrence, characterized by the principle of mutually assured destruction (MAD).

During the Cold War, nuclear diplomacy revolved around arms control agreements, such as the Strategic Arms Limitation Talks (SALT) and the Treaty on the Non-Proliferation of Nuclear Weapons (NPT). These negotiations aimed to prevent the spread of nuclear weapons, reduce the risk of accidental war, and foster stability between the superpowers.

The end of the Cold War brought about a new era in nuclear diplomacy. With the collapse of the Soviet Union, the focus shifted to disarmament and non-proliferation efforts. The Comprehensive Nuclear-Test-Ban Treaty (CTBT) and the START treaties marked significant milestones in this regard.

However, nuclear diplomacy has not been without its challenges. The emergence of new nuclear states, such as India, Pakistan, and North Korea, posed significant hurdles to disarmament efforts. The nuclear aspirations of these countries have strained international relations and complicated the nuclear non-proliferation regime.

Moreover, nuclear accidents and incidents, such as the Chernobyl and Fukushima disasters, have underscored the importance of nuclear safety and emergency preparedness. International cooperation and diplomacy have been crucial in addressing these incidents and mitigating their consequences.

In recent years, technological advancements and modernization efforts have added another layer of complexity to nuclear diplomacy. The development of advanced delivery systems, like ballistic missiles and nuclear submarines, has raised concerns about strategic stability and the potential for an arms race.

Furthermore, the threat of nuclear espionage and intelligence gathering has highlighted the need for robust diplomatic engagements and cooperation in preventing the proliferation of sensitive nuclear technologies.

In conclusion, nuclear diplomacy has been a crucial component of international relations, shaping the world order and influencing the behavior of states. From the Cold War era to the present, nuclear diplomacy has evolved to address changing geopolitical dynamics, technological advancements, and the challenges posed by nuclear accidents and incidents. As we navigate the complexities of the nuclear age, diplomatic efforts must continue to prioritize disarmament, non-proliferation, and nuclear safety to ensure a secure and peaceful world.

International Organizations and Treaties Promoting Nuclear Cooperation

In a world where nuclear capabilities hold immense power and potential for both destruction and development, international organizations and treaties play a crucial role in promoting nuclear cooperation among nations. These organizations and agreements aim to foster peaceful use of nuclear energy, prevent the proliferation of nuclear weapons, and ensure the safety and security of nuclear facilities worldwide. This subchapter explores the key international organizations and treaties that are at the forefront of promoting nuclear cooperation.

One of the most prominent organizations in this realm is the International Atomic Energy Agency (IAEA). Established in 1957, the IAEA serves as the global watchdog for the peaceful use of nuclear energy. Its primary objective is to prevent the spread of nuclear weapons by verifying that countries adhere to their commitments under the Treaty on the Non-Proliferation of Nuclear Weapons (NPT). The IAEA also provides technical assistance and expertise to countries seeking to develop nuclear energy for peaceful purposes.

The NPT, signed in 1968, remains the cornerstone of nuclear non-proliferation efforts. It aims to prevent the spread of nuclear weapons, promote disarmament, and enable the peaceful use of nuclear energy. Under the treaty, non-nuclear weapon states commit not to acquire nuclear weapons, while nuclear weapon states commit to disarmament. The NPT has been instrumental in curbing the proliferation of nuclear weapons and encouraging countries to pursue peaceful nuclear energy programs.

Another significant treaty is the Comprehensive Nuclear-Test-Ban Treaty (CTBT), which prohibits all forms of nuclear weapons testing. Although the treaty has not yet entered into force, it has garnered widespread support and serves as a norm against nuclear testing. The CTBT's verification regime, which includes a global network of monitoring stations, helps detect and deter any clandestine nuclear weapons testing.

Additionally, the Nuclear Suppliers Group (NSG) plays a crucial role in controlling the export of nuclear materials and technology. Established in 1975, the NSG aims to ensure that nuclear exports are used solely for peaceful purposes and do not contribute to the development of nuclear weapons. Its guidelines help member states regulate their nuclear exports and prevent the misuse of sensitive technologies.

These international organizations and treaties serve as vital mechanisms for promoting nuclear cooperation and addressing various nuclear-related concerns. From preventing the spread of nuclear weapons to ensuring the safe operation of nuclear power plants, their efforts contribute to global nuclear security and stability. By fostering dialogue, transparency, and cooperation, these organizations and treaties play a pivotal role in shaping the future of nuclear capabilities and their impact on the world.

In conclusion, international organizations like the IAEA, treaties such as the NPT and CTBT, and groups like the NSG are instrumental in promoting nuclear cooperation among nations. These entities address various aspects of nuclear capabilities, including disarmament, non-proliferation, safety, and peaceful use of nuclear energy. As the world grapples with the opportunities and challenges posed by nuclear capabilities, these international organizations and treaties continue to play a vital role in shaping the global nuclear landscape.

Nuclear Standoffs and Diplomatic Crises

In the realm of international relations, nuclear standoffs and diplomatic crises have become critical issues that demand our attention. This subchapter delves into the complex world of nuclear politics, examining how nuclear capabilities and aspirations shape global dynamics and influence diplomatic relations.

Nuclear standoffs, characterized by heightened tensions between nuclear-armed states, pose significant threats to global security. The possession of nuclear weapons grants states immense power, but it also poses the risk of triggering a catastrophic conflict. Deterrence theory, a key concept in understanding nuclear standoffs, argues that possessing nuclear weapons prevents adversaries from launching an attack due to the fear of retaliation. However, the delicate balance of power can easily be disrupted, leading to potential crises and conflicts.

Diplomatic crises, arising from nuclear ambitions and disputes, showcase the intricate web of relationships between nations. Aspirants to the nuclear club, countries seeking to acquire nuclear capabilities, often face resistance from the international community. These aspirations can lead to diplomatic crises, as seen in the cases of North Korea and Iran. The pursuit of nuclear weapons by these states has strained relations and triggered sanctions and negotiations.

Conversely, some countries have made the commendable decision to publicly renounce nuclear weapons. These acts of disarmament promote global peace and stability, fostering trust and cooperation among nations. However, such renunciations can also create diplomatic challenges, as countries must navigate the delicate balance between maintaining security and assuaging concerns of allies.

Nuclear diplomacy plays a crucial role in managing these tensions and crises. International agreements and organizations, such as the Treaty on the Non-Proliferation of Nuclear Weapons and the International Atomic Energy Agency, serve as avenues for diplomatic negotiations and cooperation. These forums enable states to address concerns, share information, and work towards disarmament and non-proliferation.

Moreover, nuclear safety and emergency preparedness are paramount in the face of potential accidents and incidents. Lessons learned from past catastrophes, such as Chernobyl and Fukushima, underscore the importance of robust safety measures and international cooperation in preventing and mitigating nuclear disasters.

Overall, this subchapter highlights the intricate interplay between nuclear standoffs, diplomatic crises, and global security. By examining the complexities of nuclear politics and the efforts towards disarmament, non-proliferation, and safety, we gain insight into the challenges and opportunities facing the international community in the nuclear age.

Chapter 8: Nuclear Deterrence and Strategic Stability

The Concept of Nuclear Deterrence

Nuclear deterrence is a fundamental concept in the realm of international relations and the use of nuclear weapons. It refers to the strategy of preventing a nuclear attack by maintaining a credible threat of retaliation. This subchapter aims to explain the concept of nuclear deterrence and its significance in maintaining strategic stability among nations.

Nuclear deterrence is built on the principle of mutually assured destruction (MAD). The idea behind MAD is that if two or more nations possess nuclear weapons and the capability to deliver them, an attack on one would result in a devastating retaliation on the attacker. This creates a situation where both sides have a strong incentive to avoid initiating a nuclear conflict.

Deterrence operates on the assumption that the potential costs of a nuclear attack outweigh any perceived benefits. By possessing a robust nuclear arsenal, a country can dissuade potential adversaries from launching an attack. This is based on the belief that no rational actor would willingly engage in actions that would lead to their own destruction.

The concept of nuclear deterrence has been a driving force behind the proliferation of nuclear weapons. Currently, there are several countries with nuclear capabilities, including the United States, Russia, China, France, the United Kingdom, India, Pakistan, Israel, and North Korea. These countries, known as the Nuclear Club, rely on the concept of deterrence to maintain their security and protect their national interests.

However, the concept of nuclear deterrence is not without controversy. Critics argue that it creates a dangerous and unstable world, where any miscalculation or misinterpretation of intentions could lead to a catastrophic nuclear exchange. They advocate for nuclear disarmament and non-proliferation efforts, aiming to reduce the number of nuclear weapons and eventually eliminate them altogether.

Despite the ongoing debate, nuclear deterrence has played a significant role in preventing major conflicts since the end of World War II. It has contributed to the stability of the international system by establishing a delicate balance of power among nuclear-armed states. However, it is crucial to continue exploring diplomatic avenues and promoting peaceful resolutions to conflicts to reduce reliance on nuclear weapons.

In conclusion, the concept of nuclear deterrence is a central element in the realm of nuclear capabilities. It aims to prevent a nuclear attack by maintaining a credible threat of retaliation. While it has its detractors, nuclear deterrence has contributed to strategic stability among nations with nuclear capabilities. Nonetheless, efforts to promote nuclear disarmament and non-proliferation remain essential in creating a safer and more peaceful world.

Nuclear Arsenals and Strategic Stability

In today's world, the issue of nuclear arsenals and strategic stability has become an increasingly important topic of discussion. The possession and development of nuclear weapons by certain countries have raised concerns about the potential consequences and implications for global security. This subchapter aims to provide an overview of nuclear arsenals and their impact on strategic stability, addressing the interests of the public and various niches, including the nuclear club, aspirants, and those who have renounced nuclear capabilities.

Nuclear weapons have been a defining feature of international relations since the end of World War II. The nuclear club, consisting of countries such as the United States, Russia, China, France, and the United Kingdom, possess significant nuclear arsenals. These countries have developed sophisticated delivery systems, including missiles, submarines, and bombers, which enhance their deterrence capabilities.

However, the possession of nuclear weapons also raises concerns about strategic stability. The threat of a nuclear exchange between two nuclear-armed states can lead to a dangerous escalation spiral, potentially resulting in catastrophic consequences for humanity. Therefore, efforts to prevent the use of nuclear weapons and maintain strategic stability have become crucial.

Nuclear disarmament and non-proliferation efforts play a pivotal role in reducing the risks associated with nuclear arsenals. International treaties such as the Treaty on the Non-Proliferation of Nuclear Weapons (NPT) aim to prevent the spread of nuclear weapons and encourage disarmament. These treaties are essential tools for promoting global peace and security.

Additionally, nuclear diplomacy and international relations have a significant impact on strategic stability. The relationships and interactions between nuclear-armed states shape the global nuclear landscape. Diplomatic efforts, such as arms control agreements and confidence-building measures, contribute to reducing tensions and enhancing stability.

Moreover, nuclear safety and emergency preparedness are essential considerations in the nuclear realm. Accidents and incidents, such as Chernobyl and Fukushima, have highlighted the potential risks associated with nuclear power plants and the need for robust safety measures. Proper emergency preparedness and international cooperation are vital to prevent and respond effectively to nuclear accidents.

Furthermore, nuclear espionage and intelligence gathering have played a role in shaping the global nuclear landscape. Understanding the capabilities and intentions of other nuclear-armed states is essential for strategic planning and maintaining stability.

Lastly, advancements in technology and nuclear weapons modernization have the potential to impact strategic stability. Technological developments can lead to more accurate and lethal nuclear weapons, which may have implications for deterrence and escalation dynamics.

In conclusion, the issue of nuclear arsenals and strategic stability is of utmost importance in today's world. Understanding the complexities and challenges associated with nuclear weapons is crucial for the public, the nuclear club, aspirants, and those who have renounced nuclear capabilities. Efforts towards nuclear disarmament, non-proliferation, safety, diplomacy, and intelligence gathering are essential to ensure a more stable and secure world.

Nuclear Arms Control and its Impact on Deterrence

In the realm of international relations, the concept of nuclear deterrence has played a significant role in shaping global security dynamics for decades. Nuclear arms control, as a subset of this complex issue, has emerged as a crucial means of regulating the possession, development, and deployment of nuclear weapons. Understanding its impact on deterrence is pivotal for comprehending the delicate balance between peace and conflict in our world.

Nuclear arms control refers to the various agreements, treaties, and negotiations undertaken by states possessing nuclear capabilities to limit or reduce their arsenals. The objective is to promote strategic stability by minimizing the risk of a nuclear war. These agreements often involve the exchange of information, verification mechanisms, and confidence-building measures, creating an environment of transparency and predictability.

One of the most prominent examples of nuclear arms control is the Treaty on the Non-Proliferation of Nuclear Weapons (NPT). The NPT seeks to prevent the spread of nuclear weapons, promote disarmament, and facilitate the peaceful use of nuclear energy. By limiting the number of states with nuclear capabilities, the NPT aims to maintain a balance of power and deter potential conflicts between nuclear-armed nations.

The impact of nuclear arms control on deterrence is twofold. Firstly, it reduces the number of nuclear weapons in circulation, thereby lowering the chances of accidental or intentional nuclear war. This reduction is achieved through arms reduction treaties, such as the Strategic Arms Reduction Treaty (START) between the United States and Russia, which have significantly reduced the number of deployed nuclear warheads.

Secondly, nuclear arms control promotes trust and confidence-building measures among states. By engaging in dialogue and cooperating on disarmament efforts, countries can alleviate tensions and increase predictability in their strategic interactions. This, in turn, enhances the effectiveness of deterrence, as states have a clearer understanding of each other's intentions and capabilities.

Nevertheless, it is important to acknowledge the challenges and limitations of nuclear arms control. The pursuit of deterrence through arms control requires the participation and cooperation of all nuclear-armed states. The asymmetry in nuclear capabilities and the pursuit of technological advancements by some nations pose significant obstacles to achieving comprehensive disarmament.

Moreover, the evolving nature of nuclear weapons, including their delivery systems and technological advancements, necessitates regular updates and modernization efforts. Balancing the need for modernization with disarmament commitments is a complex task that requires careful diplomacy and negotiation.

In conclusion, nuclear arms control plays a crucial role in shaping the dynamics of deterrence in our world. By reducing the number of nuclear weapons and promoting trust among states, arms control measures contribute to strategic stability and minimize the risk of nuclear conflict. However, achieving comprehensive disarmament and addressing the complexities of modernization remain ongoing challenges that require sustained international cooperation and commitment.

Chapter 9: Nuclear Weapons Delivery Systems

Ballistic Missiles: Land-based and Submarine-launched

In the realm of nuclear capabilities, few weapons are as synonymous with power and destruction as ballistic missiles. These missiles serve as the backbone of a country's nuclear arsenal, capable of delivering devastating nuclear warheads with pinpoint accuracy. In this subchapter, we will delve into the two primary types of ballistic missiles: land-based and submarine-launched.

Land-based ballistic missiles are stationed on solid ground, typically in underground silos or mobile launchers. These missiles offer several advantages, including their ability to be easily maintained and monitored. Land-based missiles can be deployed in fixed locations, making them a visible deterrent to potential adversaries. Countries like the United States, Russia, and China possess formidable land-based missile systems, serving as a crucial component of their nuclear deterrence strategy.

On the other hand, submarine-launched ballistic missiles (SLBMs) offer a different level of flexibility and stealth. These missiles are launched from submarines submerged beneath the ocean's surface, making them incredibly difficult to detect and intercept. Submarines equipped with SLBMs can patrol vast stretches of the world's oceans, remaining hidden and ready to strike at a moment's notice. Notable examples of nations with submarine-launched ballistic missiles include the United States, Russia, the United Kingdom, France, and China.

Both land-based and submarine-launched ballistic missiles play a vital role in maintaining strategic stability and deterrence. The possession of these missiles serves as a deterrent against potential adversaries, ensuring that any act of aggression would result in devastating retaliation. The global nuclear landscape is heavily influenced by the presence of these missile systems, with countries carefully considering the balance of power and the potential consequences before taking any military action.

However, it is crucial to acknowledge the risks associated with ballistic missiles. Accidental launches, mechanical failures, or unauthorized access to these weapons can result in catastrophic consequences. Therefore, robust safety protocols, emergency preparedness measures, and international cooperation are essential in minimizing the risks associated with these weapons.

Understanding the capabilities and intricacies of ballistic missiles is vital for anyone interested in nuclear matters. Whether you are a member of the public seeking knowledge on international relations, a nuclear power plant operator concerned about national security, or an advocate for nuclear disarmament, comprehending the role of ballistic missiles is crucial. By exploring this topic, we can better grasp the complexities of nuclear deterrence, the challenges of nuclear safety, and the implications of technological advancements in the field of nuclear weaponry.

Strategic Bombers and Nuclear Weapons

Strategic bombers play a crucial role in the complex world of nuclear weapons. In this subchapter, we will explore the significance of strategic bombers in the context of nuclear capabilities, their role in nuclear deterrence, and the advancements in technology that have shaped their development.

Strategic bombers are long-range aircraft designed to carry and deliver nuclear weapons. These bombers serve as one of the three primary delivery systems for nuclear weapons, alongside missiles and submarines. The ability to strike targets from the air provides a unique flexibility and versatility to a country's nuclear arsenal. While missiles and submarines offer their own advantages, strategic bombers offer the advantage of being able to change targets mid-flight and provide a visible display of a nation's nuclear capabilities. This visible display can be a potent tool for deterrence and a means of shaping international relations.

The use of strategic bombers as a nuclear deterrent dates back to the Cold War, where both the United States and the Soviet Union relied heavily on these aircraft. The concept of mutually assured destruction (MAD) emerged, where the possession of a credible and survivable nuclear arsenal was believed to deter potential adversaries from launching a first strike. Strategic bombers formed a critical part of this deterrence strategy, as they provided a visible and mobile platform for delivering nuclear weapons.

Advancements in technology have significantly impacted the capabilities of strategic bombers. These advancements include increased range, stealth capabilities, and improved precision in delivering nuclear weapons. The development of supersonic bombers, such as the B-1B Lancer and the Russian Tu-160, has further enhanced their effectiveness. Additionally, the integration of advanced communication and surveillance systems has made strategic bombers even more capable and reliable in the modern era.

However, the role of strategic bombers extends beyond nuclear deterrence. These aircraft can also be used in conventional operations, such as long-range precision strikes or aerial reconnaissance. This flexibility allows countries to utilize their strategic bombers for a variety of purposes, making them a valuable asset in both nuclear and non-nuclear scenarios.

In conclusion, strategic bombers play a critical role in a country's nuclear capabilities. These aircraft serve as a visible display of a nation's nuclear deterrent, offering flexibility and versatility in delivering nuclear weapons. Advancements in technology have further enhanced the capabilities of strategic bombers, making them even more effective in the modern era. Understanding the role of strategic bombers is crucial for comprehending the complex dynamics of nuclear weapons and their impact on international relations.

Emerging Technologies in Nuclear Weapons Delivery

The rapid advancements in technology have not only revolutionized various industries but have also had a significant impact on nuclear weapons delivery systems. In this subchapter, we will explore the emerging technologies that are shaping the future of nuclear weapons delivery and the implications they have on global security.

One of the most notable advancements in this field is the development of hypersonic missiles. Hypersonic missiles can travel at speeds exceeding Mach 5, making them extremely difficult to intercept. These missiles can be equipped with nuclear warheads, posing a significant challenge to existing missile defense systems. The development of hypersonic technology by countries such as the United States, Russia, and China has raised concerns about the potential for a new arms race and increased instability in international relations.

Another emerging technology is the use of unmanned underwater vehicles (UUVs) for nuclear weapons delivery. These UUVs can navigate autonomously and carry nuclear warheads, posing a new threat to maritime security. The use of UUVs allows countries to deploy nuclear weapons in a stealthy and covert manner, making detection and interception even more challenging.

Advancements in artificial intelligence (AI) and machine learning are also playing a significant role in nuclear weapons delivery systems. AI can enhance the accuracy and effectiveness of missile guidance systems, making them more capable of evading missile defense systems. However, the use of AI in nuclear weapons delivery raises ethical concerns, as it may lead to automated decision-making processes that could escalate conflicts.

Furthermore, the development of space-based delivery systems is gaining attention. Satellites equipped with nuclear warheads can be deployed in space and reenter the Earth's atmosphere, targeting specific locations with high precision. This technology poses new challenges for arms control efforts and strategic stability, as it can bypass traditional missile defense systems.

As these emerging technologies continue to evolve, it is crucial for the public and policymakers to understand their implications. The potential for increased strategic instability, arms races, and the challenges they pose to arms control and non-proliferation efforts cannot be ignored. It is essential to engage in informed discussions and promote transparency to ensure that these technologies are used responsibly and in the interest of global security.

In conclusion, the emergence of hypersonic missiles, unmanned underwater vehicles, AI, and space-based delivery systems are reshaping the landscape of nuclear weapons delivery. The implications of these technologies on global security, arms control efforts, and international relations cannot be understated. It is imperative for the public to be aware of these advancements and engage in discussions to ensure responsible use and effective regulation in this rapidly evolving field.

Chapter 10: Nuclear Weapons Modernization and Technological Advancements

Modernization Programs of Nuclear Weapons States

In the fast-paced and ever-evolving world of nuclear weapons, it is crucial to stay informed about the modernization programs of nuclear weapons states. These programs have significant implications for international security, nuclear disarmament efforts, and the overall stability of the world order. In this subchapter, we will delve into the modernization efforts undertaken by various nuclear weapons states and their impact on global affairs.

Nuclear weapons states, such as the United States, Russia, China, France, and the United Kingdom, have consistently invested in their arsenals to maintain a credible deterrent and ensure their weapons remain effective. Modernization efforts primarily focus on three key areas: warhead development, delivery systems, and command and control infrastructure.

Regarding warhead development, nuclear weapons states invest in designing more advanced and sophisticated warheads to enhance their capabilities. This includes research on miniaturized warheads, increased accuracy, and improved reliability. It is vital to monitor these advancements as they have implications for non-proliferation efforts and can potentially trigger arms races among aspiring nuclear states.

Delivery systems play a pivotal role in the effectiveness of nuclear weapons. Modernization efforts involve developing advanced missiles, submarines, and bombers capable of delivering warheads accurately and evading enemy defenses. The evolution of these delivery systems can significantly impact strategic stability and international relations, as it alters the balance of power between nuclear-armed states.

Alongside warhead development and delivery systems, nuclear weapons states also invest in upgrading their command and control infrastructure. This ensures seamless communication, decision-making, and coordination in times of crisis. Upgrades in this area aim to enhance the survivability and reliability of nuclear weapons systems, thereby reinforcing the credibility of deterrent capabilities.

The modernization programs of nuclear weapons states have generated debates and concerns within the public and various interest groups. Advocates argue that modernization ensures the safety, effectiveness, and reliability of existing nuclear arsenals, which contributes to deterrence and strategic stability. Critics, however, express concerns about the escalating costs, potential for arms races, and the impact on disarmament efforts.

Understanding the modernization programs of nuclear weapons states is crucial for all stakeholders, including the public, nuclear-capable countries, aspiring nuclear states, and those who renounced nuclear weapons. It enables informed discussions on nuclear disarmament and non-proliferation efforts, nuclear safety and emergency preparedness, and the broader implications for international relations and global security.

By examining the advancements in nuclear weapons technology, delivery systems, and command and control infrastructure, we can better comprehend the complexities and challenges associated with nuclear weapons. This knowledge empowers individuals to engage in informed discussions and contribute to shaping policies that promote peace, security, and responsible nuclear governance on a global scale.

Miniaturization and Precision in Nuclear Weapons

In the world of nuclear weapons, the concepts of miniaturization and precision play a crucial role. These advancements have been at the forefront of technological developments in recent years, shaping the landscape of global security. In this subchapter, we will delve into the intricacies of miniaturization and precision in nuclear weapons, their implications, and their impact on the international stage.

Miniaturization is the process of reducing the size and weight of nuclear warheads while maintaining their destructive power. This development has significant implications for the countries possessing nuclear capabilities, as it allows for a more flexible and versatile nuclear arsenal. Smaller warheads can be deployed on a wider range of delivery systems, including missiles, submarines, and bombers. This capability enhances a nation's ability to project power and serves as a deterrent against potential adversaries.

Precision, on the other hand, refers to the accuracy of nuclear weapons in hitting their intended targets with minimal collateral damage. Precision-guided systems enable more precise targeting, reducing the risk of unintended casualties and destruction. This advancement has revolutionized the strategic landscape, as it enables countries to employ nuclear weapons with greater precision and confidence.

The miniaturization and precision of nuclear weapons have far-reaching implications for the nuclear club, aspirant nations, and those who have publicly renounced nuclear capabilities. For the nuclear club, these advancements enhance their nuclear deterrent capabilities and provide them with a more credible and effective means of defense. Aspiring nations may be enticed by the potential benefits of miniaturized and precise nuclear weapons, leading to increased proliferation concerns. Meanwhile, countries that have renounced nuclear capabilities may find themselves at a disadvantage, as they are unable to leverage these advancements for their national security.

The development of miniaturization and precision in nuclear weapons also raises concerns about nuclear safety, emergency preparedness, and non-proliferation efforts. The smaller size of warheads may increase the risk of accidents or unauthorized use, necessitating robust safety measures and emergency response protocols. Additionally, the potential for precision strikes may lead to a heightened fear of nuclear escalation during conflicts.

In conclusion, miniaturization and precision are key factors shaping the landscape of nuclear weapons. These advancements offer both benefits and challenges for countries with nuclear capabilities, those aspiring to possess them, and those who have renounced them. It is crucial for the international community to closely monitor these developments, ensuring that nuclear weapons are only used as a last resort and that efforts towards disarmament and non-proliferation remain at the forefront of global security initiatives.

The Challenges of Technological Advancements

Technological advancements have revolutionized every aspect of human life, from communication and transportation to healthcare and entertainment. However, these advancements also bring with them a unique set of challenges, particularly in the realm of nuclear capabilities. In this subchapter, we will explore the various challenges posed by technological advancements in the context of countries with nuclear capabilities.

One of the primary challenges is nuclear safety and emergency preparedness. As countries develop more advanced nuclear power plants and increase their energy production capabilities, the risk of accidents and incidents also rises. Events like the Chernobyl and Fukushima disasters have highlighted the devastating consequences of nuclear accidents, not only in terms of human lives but also the long-term environmental and economic impact. It is crucial for countries to invest in robust safety measures, emergency response protocols, and transparent reporting to mitigate these risks.

Furthermore, technological advancements in nuclear weapons testing and development present significant challenges to global non-proliferation efforts. As countries strive to modernize their nuclear arsenals, there is a risk of triggering an arms race and increasing tensions among nations. Efforts to curb the spread of nuclear weapons and promote disarmament become more complicated in the face of these advancements. Effective diplomacy and international cooperation are essential to address these challenges and maintain global peace and security.

Additionally, nuclear espionage and intelligence gathering have become more sophisticated with technological advancements. Countries with nuclear capabilities must be vigilant in protecting their sensitive information, as the theft of such knowledge can have severe consequences for national security. Strengthening cybersecurity measures and enhancing intelligence capabilities are crucial in countering these threats.

Moreover, the advancement of nuclear weapons delivery systems, such as missiles, submarines, and bombers, adds another layer of complexity to international relations. The development of more advanced and efficient delivery systems can disrupt the existing balance of power and lead to increased tensions between nuclear-capable nations. Striking a delicate balance between deterrence and strategic stability becomes even more challenging in this evolving technological landscape.

Lastly, the nuclear weapons modernization and technological advancements also raise concerns about the potential for accidental or unauthorized use. As countries upgrade their nuclear arsenals with more sophisticated and precise weapons, there is an increased risk of miscalculations or technical malfunctions that could potentially lead to a catastrophic event. Robust command and control systems, strict safeguards, and thorough training of personnel are vital in ensuring the safe and responsible use of nuclear weapons.

In conclusion, while technological advancements in the field of nuclear capabilities offer numerous benefits, they also bring forth significant challenges. From ensuring nuclear safety and emergency preparedness to managing international relations and preventing nuclear proliferation, countries with nuclear capabilities must navigate this complex landscape with caution and responsibility. By addressing these challenges head-on, we can strive towards a world where the benefits of technological advancements are harnessed without compromising global peace and security.

Chapter 11: Nuclear Espionage and Intelligence Gathering

Historical Cases of Nuclear Espionage

Nuclear espionage has been a significant concern in the world of international relations and national security since the development of nuclear weapons. As countries sought to gain an edge in the nuclear arms race, the clandestine acquisition of nuclear technology and information became a crucial part of their strategies. This subchapter will delve into some of the most notable historical cases of nuclear espionage, shedding light on the lengths to which countries have gone to obtain nuclear secrets.

One of the earliest instances of nuclear espionage occurred during World War II. The Manhattan Project, which aimed to develop the atomic bomb, was a top-secret operation conducted by the United States. However, Soviet intelligence managed to infiltrate the project and gather valuable information. The most famous spy in this case was Klaus Fuchs, a German physicist working on the project who passed classified information to the Soviet Union. This infiltration significantly accelerated the Soviet Union's own nuclear weapons program.

Another historic case of nuclear espionage involved Israel's acquisition of nuclear technology. In the 1960s and 1970s, Israeli intelligence managed to infiltrate various nuclear facilities around the world, most notably in France and the United States. This enabled Israel to develop its own nuclear weapons program, which it has never officially acknowledged.

More recently, the case of Pakistani scientist Abdul Qadeer Khan brought nuclear espionage back into the spotlight. Khan, once hailed as the father of Pakistan's nuclear program, was found to have been involved in an extensive black-market network that supplied nuclear technology to countries such as Iran and North Korea. This case exposed the vulnerabilities in the global non-proliferation regime and highlighted the difficulties in preventing the spread of nuclear technology.

These historical cases of nuclear espionage demonstrate the high stakes involved in the acquisition of nuclear weapons technology. They also underscore the importance of robust intelligence gathering and counterintelligence efforts by countries to protect their national security interests. The consequences of nuclear espionage can be far-reaching, not only in terms of regional security but also in the risks of nuclear proliferation and the potential for nuclear accidents.

As the world continues to grapple with the challenges posed by nuclear weapons, it is crucial for nations to remain vigilant in their efforts to prevent nuclear espionage. Through international cooperation, intelligence sharing, and the strengthening of non-proliferation mechanisms, the global community can work towards a safer and more secure world, free from the threats posed by the illicit acquisition of nuclear technology.

Espionage Techniques and Countermeasures

In the world of nuclear capabilities, espionage and intelligence gathering play a crucial role. This subchapter aims to shed light on the various espionage techniques employed by nations with nuclear capabilities, as well as the countermeasures taken to protect sensitive information.

Espionage, the act of obtaining confidential information without the owner's permission, has been a long-standing practice among nations. When it comes to nuclear capabilities, countries are constantly striving to gain an upper hand by gathering classified intelligence. This includes information related to nuclear power plants and energy production, nuclear disarmament and non-proliferation efforts, nuclear weapons testing and development, nuclear safety and emergency preparedness, nuclear diplomacy and international relations, nuclear deterrence and strategic stability, nuclear weapons delivery systems, nuclear weapons modernization and technological advancements, and even nuclear accidents and incidents.

Espionage techniques can vary from traditional methods to sophisticated cyber espionage. Traditional methods involve human intelligence, where agents are deployed to gather information through covert operations, surveillance, and infiltration. These agents may operate within the target country's government, military, or even within the nuclear facilities themselves.

Cyber espionage, on the other hand, involves the use of advanced hacking techniques to gain unauthorized access to computer networks and systems. This allows spies to steal classified information or disrupt nuclear operations. The rise of cyber threats has made it imperative for nations to invest heavily in cybersecurity to safeguard their sensitive nuclear data.

To counter these espionage techniques, countries with nuclear capabilities employ a range of countermeasures. These include strict background checks and security clearances for personnel working in sensitive positions. Physical security measures, such as surveillance systems, access control, and secure storage facilities, are implemented to protect nuclear facilities from unauthorized access.

Furthermore, advanced encryption methods and secure communication networks are used to safeguard classified information. Regular security audits and training programs are conducted to ensure the effectiveness of these countermeasures.

In conclusion, espionage is a constant threat to countries with nuclear capabilities. Understanding the various espionage techniques employed and implementing robust countermeasures is crucial to protect sensitive information related to nuclear power, weapons, and safety. By staying vigilant and investing in cybersecurity, nations can mitigate the risks associated with nuclear espionage and maintain the security of their nuclear capabilities.

Cyber Espionage and Nuclear Weapons

In today's digitized world, the threat of cyber espionage has become a pressing concern, particularly when it intersects with the realm of nuclear weapons. This subchapter aims to shed light on the intricate relationship between cyber espionage and nuclear weapons, exploring the potential risks, challenges, and implications for both current nuclear powers and those aspiring to possess such capabilities.

Cyber espionage involves the unauthorized access, extraction, and manipulation of sensitive information through digital means. When it comes to nuclear weapons, the stakes are incredibly high. The theft of classified data related to nuclear technology, weapons development, or even strategic plans could have catastrophic consequences. Therefore, it is crucial for all countries with nuclear capabilities to prioritize cybersecurity and safeguard their nuclear assets from potential cyber threats.

One major concern is the possibility of cyber attacks targeting nuclear power plants and energy production facilities. Such attacks could disrupt operations, compromise safety measures, or even lead to a catastrophic accident. Therefore, governments and nuclear power plant operators must invest in robust cybersecurity measures to prevent unauthorized access and ensure the safety of these facilities.

Furthermore, cyber espionage can also be used as a means to gather intelligence on nuclear weapons testing and development. In an era where technological advancements are rapidly evolving, the theft of classified information related to nuclear research can significantly accelerate the progress of aspiring nuclear powers. This poses a significant challenge for countries committed to non-proliferation efforts, as it becomes harder to monitor and control the spread of nuclear weapons technology.

Nuclear diplomacy and international relations are also deeply affected by cyber espionage. Unauthorized access to diplomatic communications or classified negotiations can undermine trust and compromise the integrity of diplomatic efforts to promote nuclear disarmament and non-proliferation. Therefore, ensuring the cybersecurity of diplomatic channels is of utmost importance for maintaining stability and fostering cooperation among nuclear powers and aspiring nations.

Moreover, cyber espionage can also target the technological advancements and modernization of nuclear weapons delivery systems. This includes missiles, submarines, and bombers. By gaining access to classified data, malicious actors can exploit vulnerabilities in these systems, potentially compromising their reliability and effectiveness. This underscores the imperative need for constant vigilance and investment in cybersecurity to counter such threats.

In conclusion, cyber espionage poses significant challenges in the realm of nuclear weapons. It threatens the security, stability, and safety of both current nuclear powers and those aspiring to possess such capabilities. Governments, nuclear power plant operators, and international bodies must collaborate to develop robust cybersecurity measures, promote non-proliferation efforts, and safeguard against potential cyber threats. By doing so, we can mitigate the risks associated with cyber espionage and protect our world from the catastrophic consequences of nuclear weapons falling into the wrong hands.

Chapter 12: Nuclear Accidents and Incidents

Chernobyl Disaster: Causes and Aftermath

The Chernobyl Disaster is one of the most catastrophic nuclear accidents in history, and its causes and aftermath continue to have significant implications for the global community. This subchapter explores the events leading up to the disaster, its immediate consequences, and the long-term effects on nuclear power, safety, and international relations.

On April 26, 1986, the Chernobyl Nuclear Power Plant, located in the Soviet Union (now Ukraine), experienced a catastrophic explosion and subsequent fire in Reactor 4. The accident was primarily caused by a combination of design flaws, inadequate safety measures, and human error during a safety test. The explosion released a massive amount of radioactive material into the atmosphere, contaminating the surrounding environment and exposing thousands of people to dangerous levels of radiation.

In the immediate aftermath, the Soviet authorities struggled to contain the disaster and provide accurate information to the public. The nearby town of Pripyat was evacuated, and a 30-kilometer exclusion zone was established around the plant. The health effects on the exposed population were severe, with increased rates of cancer, birth defects, and other radiation-related illnesses observed for years after the accident.

The Chernobyl Disaster had far-reaching implications beyond the immediate region. It highlighted the inherent dangers of nuclear power and raised concerns about the safety of other nuclear facilities worldwide. The incident led to significant changes in nuclear safety regulations, prompting countries to reassess their emergency preparedness and risk management protocols.

Moreover, the Chernobyl Disaster had a profound impact on nuclear diplomacy and international relations. The event exposed the Soviet Union's lack of transparency and accountability in managing nuclear accidents, leading to increased scrutiny and pressure for greater openness in the global nuclear community. It also influenced the discourse on nuclear disarmament and non-proliferation efforts, as countries recognized the potential consequences of uncontrolled nuclear incidents.

The Chernobyl Disaster also served as a stark reminder of the potential dangers of nuclear weapons. It drew attention to the risks associated with nuclear weapons testing and development, highlighting the need for international cooperation and agreements to prevent further catastrophic accidents.

In conclusion, the Chernobyl Disaster was a seminal event in the history of nuclear power and its implications continue to resonate today. It underscored the importance of nuclear safety, emergency preparedness, and international cooperation in managing the risks associated with nuclear energy and weapons. By examining the causes and aftermath of this tragic event, we can learn valuable lessons that inform our approach to nuclear power, disarmament, and global security.

Fukushima Nuclear Disaster: Lessons Learned

The Fukushima Nuclear Disaster, which occurred on March 11, 2011, was a wake-up call for the world regarding the potential dangers and risks associated with nuclear power. This subchapter titled "Fukushima Nuclear Disaster: Lessons Learned" aims to shed light on the lessons that can be derived from this catastrophic event and how they have shaped the way we view nuclear power today.

The Fukushima Daiichi nuclear power plant, located in Japan, was hit by a massive earthquake and subsequent tsunami, leading to a series of meltdowns in three of its reactors. The disaster not only resulted in the release of radioactive material into the environment but also had far-reaching consequences on public health, the economy, and the perception of nuclear power around the world.

One of the most significant lessons learned from Fukushima is the importance of robust safety measures and emergency preparedness. The disaster highlighted the need for comprehensive risk assessments, updated safety protocols, and effective evacuation plans. Governments and regulatory bodies globally have since taken steps to enhance safety standards at nuclear power plants to prevent similar incidents in the future.

Furthermore, the Fukushima disaster underscored the importance of transparency and effective communication during nuclear emergencies. The initial response to the crisis was marred by confusion and contradictory information, leading to public distrust and panic. As a result, governments and nuclear operators now prioritize open and honest communication with the public, ensuring that accurate and timely information is disseminated during crises.

Additionally, Fukushima demonstrated the significance of international collaboration and cooperation in addressing nuclear emergencies. Following the disaster, the international community came together to provide assistance and support to Japan. This incident prompted countries to strengthen their cooperation in sharing knowledge, expertise, and resources to mitigate the impact of future nuclear accidents.

Moreover, the Fukushima disaster ignited a global debate on the future of nuclear power. While some countries decided to phase out their nuclear energy programs, others recognized the importance of nuclear power as a low-carbon energy source and focused on improving safety measures. The incident served as a catalyst for countries to reassess their energy policies and explore alternative sources of energy to reduce reliance on nuclear power.

In conclusion, the Fukushima Nuclear Disaster has left an indelible mark on the world, prompting important lessons to be learned. The incident has led to enhanced safety measures, improved emergency preparedness, and increased international cooperation. It has also sparked a global dialogue on the role of nuclear power in our energy future. By learning from the mistakes of the past, we can strive for a safer and more sustainable future in the realm of nuclear power.

Other Nuclear Accidents and Near Misses

While the world has witnessed major nuclear accidents such as Chernobyl and Fukushima, there have been several other incidents and near misses that highlight the importance of nuclear safety and emergency preparedness. This subchapter explores some of these lesser-known events and their implications for the public, the nuclear club countries, aspirants, and those who publicly renounced nuclear capabilities.

One such incident occurred in 1957 in Kyshtym, Soviet Union (now Russia), at the Mayak Production Association. A cooling system failure led to a chemical explosion, releasing a significant amount of radioactive material into the atmosphere. The incident was kept secret by Soviet authorities, causing widespread contamination and health issues for the surrounding population. This incident serves as a reminder that transparency and open communication are essential in preventing and mitigating the consequences of nuclear accidents.

Another near miss took place in 1980 at the Titan II missile complex in Arkansas, United States. A maintenance worker dropped a wrench, which punctured the fuel tank of a missile, resulting in the release of highly toxic rocket fuel. The incident led to the evacuation of nearby residents and highlighted the potential dangers of nuclear weapons even during routine operations.

In 1999, a criticality accident occurred at the Tokaimura nuclear fuel processing facility in Japan. Due to a series of human errors and safety violations, a nuclear chain reaction started inside a processing tank, releasing a significant amount of radiation. Two workers died from acute radiation sickness, and hundreds of others were exposed to varying levels of radiation. This incident exposed the vulnerabilities of nuclear facilities and the importance of strict adherence to safety protocols.

These incidents and near misses underline the need for continuous vigilance and improvement in nuclear safety measures. The nuclear club countries, aspirants, and those who have renounced nuclear capabilities must prioritize investment in advanced technologies and training to prevent accidents and minimize their consequences.

The public also has a role to play in nuclear safety. By staying informed about the risks associated with nuclear power and weapons, individuals can advocate for stricter safety regulations, transparency, and emergency preparedness. Public pressure can drive governments and nuclear operators to prioritize safety over other considerations.

In conclusion, nuclear accidents and near misses serve as reminders of the potential dangers associated with nuclear power and weapons. By learning from past incidents, improving safety measures, and fostering open communication, the nuclear club countries, aspirants, and those who publicly renounced nuclear capabilities can work towards a safer and more secure nuclear future.